Copyright 2018 N

All writers retain copyright to their work. No duplication or reuse of any selection is allowed without the express written consent of the writer.

Any resemblance to actual persons depicted in this anthology, living or dead, is entirely coincidental.

Cover Photography
William Mays

Photo editing and Cover Design
Alexis Mays

ISBN 13: 978-1717389466

ISBN 10: 1717389465

1. Anthology. 2. Fiction – General. 3. Poetry. 4. Short Stories.

Corpus Christi Writers 2018: An Anthology

Edited by
William Mays

Forward

Bouncing around local critique groups for 20 years, I realized that most of the fine writing I was privileged to read might never make it into print. Even those who persevered to a finished product generally found a small audience, often confined to friends and family. I wanted to change that.

Welcome to a creative showcase, also known as "Corpus Christi Writers 2018: An Anthology." This Anthology gives a platform to voices in the Coastal Bend. While it is all about community, it also strives to articulate universal issues. The goal is to help connect our writers with readers around the world.

When I first started contacting my friends and posting calls for submissions, I tried to find everyone. Poets. Fiction writers. History buffs. I reached out to people who might not think of themselves as writers. If someone told me an interesting story, I asked them to write it down. When I saw someone writing at Starbucks, I approached them and told them about the anthology. If I saw a compelling Facebook post, I asked if we could use it. As submissions came in, each voice was unique, and each one offered a new perspective and became an important piece in this mosaic.

The result is a snapshot of an American community.

Some of the selections in this anthology draw their power from the rich diversity of South Texas. Others evoke the sea, the dunes, or the flat and forbidding terrain. Many have nothing to do with South Texas. The writers, all natives or residents, bind the collection together with their imaginative outlooks.

This book holds everything from fiction to poetry, and there are submissions that fall somewhere in between. The works are sorted alphabetically by last name rather than by genre or style.

I did not add labels, only writers.

William Mays

Table of contents

Cabbage of Earth by **Mandy Ashcraft**	7
We Called It Baseball by **Gerald Beckman**	16
Found Money by **Kenneth Bennight**	24
Commuting by Alan **Berecka**	36
Bedroom Blarney by **Cynthia Breeding**	38
Quillan by **Brandon Cantu/Melinda Cantu**	41
Poetry by **Robin Carstensen**	43
Sirens by **William Basileios Chriss**	47
Poetry by **Roberta Shellum Dohse**	53
Poem and short story by **Charles Etheridge**	58
The Lost King by **Devorah Fox**	64
Transplants by **Paul Gonzales**	72
Two Wolf Pups by **Scott Wayland Griffin**	78
The Wedding by **Kailey Hamauei**	81
Poetry by **Joshua Hamilton**	86
It's Five O'Clock Somewhere by **Lee Hultin**	92
One Last Performance by **Bob James**	95
Jesus Lopez by **Allyson Chavez Larkin**	98
Three Little Pigs by **Skoot Larson**	101

Pepper Cain by **Carol Mays** — 104

Judgement Day by **William Mays** — 107

Emergency by **Jim McCutchon** — 114

Poetry by **Tom Murphy** — 118

Making Friends by **Olivia Noble** — 124

Please Close the Windows by **Jose Olivarez** — 126

sometimes you're just damned by **Joel Ortiz** — 129

Poetry by **Zoe Ramos** — 131

The Lesson by **Esther Bonilla Read** — 133

Random Acts by **Mona Schroeder** — 135

On Open Water by **John Swinburn** — 139

The Life of a Ship by **Neesy Tompkins** — 146

My Desert Jay by **Ana Varela** — 150

The Book of Jake by **William Walton III** — 155

Poem and Facebook Posts by **Joseph Wilson** — 165

Mandy Ashcraft

Mandy Ashcraft lives in Corpus Christi with her husband Dustin. She has worked as a Registered Dental Hygienist for eight years, and her interests include baking, science fiction, and black tea lattes. Her favorite authors are Douglas Adams, Orson Scott Card, and Kurt Vonnegut. Mandy's first full-length novel Small Orange Fruit is available on Amazon and iBooks for fans of humorous science fiction.

Cabbage of Earth

Charlie Mathis took satisfied sips of his morning coffee as he looked out over his cabbages, seeing cabbages and only cabbages which is ideal when you're a cabbage farmer. His gaze stopped on a strange arrangement of concentric circles burned into his field; the kind you'd see in a tabloid story about UFOs. There was surely a less tabloid-worthy explanation for the symbols left in his field, his personal comfort zone insisted as he scrambled to connect a few logical dots. "Those damn teenagers!" he shouted, not referencing any particular ones as there were none living within 20 miles of his Texas property; just damn teenagers in general. Charlie was in his late thirties but his isolated cabbage-soup-rich lifestyle left him one creaky porch rocking chair short of being a crotchety old man. He didn't like to be bothered, by anyone or anything.

The optic nerve spasmed in his left eye as it landed on something else. Movement. But it wasn't teenagers. A small humanoid figure was casually shoving one of the cabbages into a -- spacecraft. Why couldn't it just be teenagers?

"Who are you? I'll sic my dogs on you! Or shoot you!" he called as he grabbed his shotgun and ran towards it, stopping suddenly when the figure turned to face him. Rather than run, it dropped to its knees and began tugging at another cabbage in the dirt, which in its small hands was comparable to a large watermelon in the hands of a man. It seemed to disregard the farmer, not in a menacing way, more of a "kindly leave me to my task of stealing your crops" sort of way. Another leafy ball was lugged to the craft; shoved into it like the carry-on bag of the last passenger to board a regional plane. The creature wasn't in a hurry. Charlie would've sicked his dogs on it if he had any dogs; the threat alone was usually sufficient, but it appeared that this time he would need actual dogs. He made a mental note to adopt a few beagles, or whatever breed would best respond to "get 'em boys!" In the meantime, he would have to "get 'em" himself. He couldn't risk anyone finding out about such a bizarre encounter; media ridicule could add red ink to his struggling finances. If profits were any lower than they already were, he might have just climbed into that spacecraft and buckled up.

"I'll shoot you!" he repeated, to no response. Not that he figured an otherworldly being would have taken English as a Second Language; Charlie wasn't a brilliant man but he wasn't exceedingly dense either. He just figured the large shotgun would pole vault over the language barrier. The figure stared at him, at the gun, and slid its slender arm into the ship to retrieve something. Charlie reacted quickly to the possibility that it was groping for a weapon, some kind of laser or anything that could send his house up in flames, and pulled his trigger. A nearby cabbage exploded. He shot a second time successfully, or unsuccessfully from the point of view of the one inhaling buckshot. It didn't scream, or try to escape. It didn't wield a weapon of its own after all. It didn't pop or fizz or explode. Another alien didn't erupt from its chest cavity. There were no lasers involved. It merely sighed, and rapidly withered to the ground, with nothing but a small notecard in its hand. A 4x6 white index card. Charlie pocketed it as he rolled the craft into his barn, and masked it with an available out-of-sight-out-of-mind shield from reality that could also be identified as a tractor cover. It wasn't as if he could recycle it. He looked at the card, covered in symbols, one of them the exact symbol that had been burned into his field a year prior. He wondered if it might be a list of directions, and if it was, his seemed to be the last stop before it reached its destination. As he dug a shallow grave for the extraterrestrial sack of Earth bullets, he wondered if he might have eventually been able to communicate with it, or if he'd have been the one being buried if he'd ventured to try. It was too late to find out; at least he was on the winning side of the dirt. Padding back to the house, he decided that what had just happened had never actually happened at all. Maybe it was a dream? The coffee grounds expired six months ago, this could be a bad reaction. Or is there such thing as a hallucinogenic cabbage fungus? He attempted to overwrite his memory of it with the words "it never happened" on a loop. He would adopt some dogs, though, in case it ever happened a second time.

He nearly heaved his expired liquid breakfast onto the index card as he scanned the front page of the newspaper. "Crop Circle Leaves Local Corn Farmer A-Maize-d" was the headline his local paper had decided on, where he just knew they'd genuinely delighted in the idea that their maize joke was also corny, and an acquaintance of his smiled in black and white. In the photo he pointed toward a charred field. An overhead view showed a peculiar symbol Charlie recognized; it was also on the index card. He felt panicked, sweaty, like he'd eaten too many jalapeños after drinking too much caffeine and his organs weren't sure what to make of the combination without resulting in something biologically volcanic. Charlie walked to the barn and pulled the tractor cover from the small craft. He pressed the door and it opened outward.

"Maybe there's something else in here, something to explain what's happening," he said aloud. He wasn't sure what he'd do if he found an answer; business aside, going public about alien contact would mean every cashier and waitress and damn teenager in Texas would ask him if he was probed for the rest of his life and it would probably even be whispered at his funeral. Here lies Charlie, who might have been probed by aliens. I wasn't probed, I was robbed, he thought to himself. The metallic spacecraft was the size of an industrial washing machine, and could accommodate the small humanoid being and about 5 of his largest, most profitable cabbages comfortably. Of those there were two, and also what appeared to be several bunches of carrots. Regular earth carrots. There wasn't a single useful piece of evidence in the craft; no maps, light sabers, or anything to probe anyone with. Unless the carrots...? No, he decided, that's not what the carrots were for. It was odd. Cabbage, carrots, and now corn? Were they studying human sources of food? His nerve endings sipped a paranoid cocktail of images depicting humans in a zoo, being fed harvested plants from their native planet, zoologists working had to recreate the human diet to toss at abductees for entertainment. He'd buried one of them, whatever they were, but the newest crop circle meant it had friends. Or at least co-workers. For the first time in a long time, he felt afraid.

"Gary," he said into his cellphone; Gary was the smiling face who was, that very morning, a-maize-d. "Gary this is Charlie. Can you talk privately? It's urgent."

There was a small bar a few miles up the road that also sold terrible burgers. They agreed to meet for drinks and possibly a terrible burger, depending on how many drinks it took for that to sound like a wise decision, gastrointestinally speaking. That day it took both men exactly two beers before taking their wise decision with extra cheese.

"Charlie, why are we drinking at 10:30 in the morning?" Gary asked, pulling at something in his burger patty that looked to Charlie like a band aid. "Are you upset about that article in the paper? It's not going to affect local business—"

"Gary, I had the same thing happen in my cabbage field. It was a different symbol, but I—" he took a swig of beer to loosen gristly meat bits wedged between his teeth, "—I saw the creature that made it. I shot it. And I took this card from it." He unfolded the index card from his front pocket. Gary reacted all too calmly to the card and the shooting, even for their level of mid-morning intoxication. "Gary, what else do you know?"

It wasn't a band aid, fortunately, in the meat patty. It was just a piece of plastic wrapping likely peeled from a cheese slice. Not exactly palatable, but certainly more hygienic, and Charlie called that a win. The old corn farmer plucked it from his burger and continued eating. "This has been happening to all of us 'round here," he said. "The Jeffreys grow those big fat radishes; their fields were covered in triangles a while back." He looked at the index card. "These actually, fourth one down." He pointed. "And those big round circles at the bottom were way out west of town in some tomatoes I think."

"So this is…a list?"

"Seems to be."

"Each crop circle or symbol was left with a different type of crop. So they were going down this list and taking some of each thing. Why?"

"Hell if I know," said Gary. "I only let the paper know so I could get that girl JoAnn's attention. You seen her around lately? Last I saw she was selling some kind of candles—"

"Don't you care?" Charlie was not a patient man.

"'Course I care, JoAnn got a boob job."

Gary was a dead end. But he'd figured out one thing from their conversation; the creatures burning symbols in their fields were following a list, marking the items they needed, and then simply hauling them off later. He flashed back on his earlier idea of human exhibits. If they were taking things they needed to sustain human life elsewhere, the next logical action would be to take the humans themselves. Or had they begun that already? Come to think of it he hadn't seen the town's only attractive female JoAnn in a while; she was worthy of being beamed up for display purposes. This human comes with enhanced features!

Parting ways with Gary and his regrettable plate of crumbs, Charlie headed out to the Jeffreys' property. The ones with the triangles and big fat radishes. They lived at the edge of town and everyone knew their name. A massive wrought iron gate with JEFFREY welded into it and solar-powered accent lighting ensured you weren't accidentally unaware of them being the fanciest growers of radishes in all the land. It was unlike anything else in their humble hometown, and the locals had taken to pretentious whispering about their alleged pretentiousness. Turns out, the flavor of irony is masked well by beer. Charlie pulled up to the gate and found it open, so he continued up the dirt road that ended at the house that root vegetables built.

A middle-aged man in shorts and a bathrobe sat on the front step reading their local paper. Gary's smiling face looked up at Charlie in black and white from the front page as he approached the man, presumably Mr. Jeffrey. He didn't look especially fancy. Maybe his robe was cashmere? Charlie wasn't sure he knew what cashmere would look like.

"Can you believe all that? About the crop circles?" Charlie asked. The man looked up at him. "Name's Charlie Mathis, I live across town. I don't mean to bother you."

"Sure I can believe it. I had crop circles. Actually I had crop triangles," he sighed. "Is that a thing? Crop triangles?"

"I suppose they could be any shape. The things making them left this card, and these symbols on it." He extended the index card. "It seems to be a list. I came to see if you had any more information."

Looking at the card, Mr. Jeffrey bit his lower lip, perplexed. "I wonder if they got all of these things yet, if it's a list like you say? Maybe they're not done?"

"You mean maybe they have other things to get on this list? Maybe some of the symbols mean— I dunno, weapons? Cows? People?"

"Could mean anything. Maybe weapons, cows, and people." Mr. Jeffrey laughed. "Or maybe the last symbol means 'you can only destroy the human race after you eat your vegetables'."

"Doesn't this worry you?" It was beginning to seem like the meeting with Gary all over again; a cholesterol-free version.

"Oh sure it terrifies me. But I'm not about to go to war with them, whatever they are. Let them have the crops. They grow back." There are always options when faced with unusual circumstances, and Jeffery seemed to have taken the "horse blinders" approach to facing this one. Don't look at them, don't look into it, and water your big fat radishes; ostentatious gates don't pay for themselves.

After about fifteen minutes of small-talk about radishes and cabbages and the weather, and also a brief mention of JoAnn 2.0, Charlie convinced Mr. Jeffrey—whose first name was Jeff which was unfortunate but easy to remember—to assist him with one thing. He asked that he simply help him make a list of what symbols locals had already quietly mentioned and strategically downplayed or, in one instance, had photographed for the front page of the local paper. They spent the afternoon calling around and drawing symbols based on verbal descriptions. The too-early beer and too-terrible burger Charlie had consumed that morning made his brain feel like it was marinating in lukewarm drippings from the meat patty.

"It looks like everything on this card matches up with

something grown around here, except one. Four circles in a row. No one has seen that one, at least no one in this area that anyone's talked to."

"So there you go," said Jeff, "the symbol that means blow up the cows or whatever you said earlier." He smiled.

"You won't be laughing if it means blow up the cows."

"So long as it doesn't mean blow up the radishes. Come on Charlie, what are you trying to do here? Stir things up? Leave it alone, maybe they'll go away."

"I want to know what's happening in this town. They seem to have targeted us for a reason. What if we could warn people?" His previous concerns of negative press and/or having to watch his CPA keep the subtract button warm on her calculator had been dropped the moment he'd realized he wasn't alone in his experience. The town in which he was born, and the one he hoped to die in but not too soon, could be under attack. It was hard to tell; what he did know was that their properties were in something's scope. There was even a handwritten list. So what was their next move?

Jeff Jeffrey tied his potentially-cashmere bathrobe around himself as he walked quietly to the kitchen. Charlie could hear him slide a wooden drawer open. He returned with a long rectangle box labelled Aluminum Foil.

"Here's your hat," he said. He tossed it down in front of his visitor. "At least that's what the rest of the country will say. You gotta let it go. We can't be known for stuff like this."

"They could be dangerous! And they know how to find us!"

The man in the bathrobe sat down. He sighed, heavily. With his right hand he picked at a label on a jar of pickled radishes. It took him several minutes to respond, in an uncomfortable silence for Charlie who was also desperately wading through a hangover.

"Do you really think we need to warn people?" he asked, finally.

"I think we do. So that maybe we can find out what it all means before it's too late."

"Warn people about what?" said a female voice as it entered the room, carried by a woman who promptly booted JoAnn off of her pedestal in Charlie's mind. Mrs. Jeffrey sat down next to her husband at the table. "I'm Mila, by the way."

"We were talking about the triangles. Charlie here has had some crop circles himself. He thinks it's a list of things they're taking. He thinks they might take people next."

Mila looked ravishingly alarmed. Beautifully terrified. Exquisitely fearful. Charlie decided he shouldn't think of her that way. She was Mrs. Jeffrey and should be merely alarmed, terrified, and fearful. "We're going to be abducted!?"

"No. We're just taking precautions. Letting people know it could happen, so they're not caught off-guard," Charlie tried to soothe her with something equally frightening but re-worded. Like putting a big orange safety cone in front of a toxic spill.

It didn't take 24 hours to ignite their quaint farm town with worry. Worry of alien invasions. Worry of abductions. Worry of probing. People never forget to mention probes in regards to anything coming from anywhere that isn't Earth, where a vast universe of possibilities seems to be whittled away to human colorectal exams. The local paper accepted Charlie's compiled information and evidence in the same quiet and understated way that a famished lion accepts a zebra. Not only had their a-maize-d farmer had this experience, much of their town had similar ones. Their town was the target of something, or someone, from another planet. Fear was rolled neatly and bound with rubber bands, tossed at the front doors of the unsuspecting locals. The zebra was picked clean.

It had been a week since the breaking news and Charlie sat with Jeff Jeffrey at the same bar he'd first met with Gary, once again eating a terrible burger. Jeff didn't have one, because he was pretentious. Or maybe because they were terrible. On an old television set, a local woman revealed to a journalist that her carrots had been dug up about eight days prior, with four circles burned into her land, and thus the last mysterious symbol on the card was identified.

"Mila wants to move," Jeff said. "Doesn't want to sit around and wait for them to come."

"That's a little extreme, I think."

"Extreme?" Jeff looked at him. "We just told the entire town to be afraid for their lives. And now it's 'extreme' if they're afraid for their lives?"

"We don't even know if they're coming back. We just told people to watch for them."

"Yeah, but you tell people to watch their backs and they panic," said Jeff as he watched Charlie mop his wet plate with the last piece of hamburger bun. "We weren't even sure we were in danger at all."

"Isn't it better to be safe than sorry?" Charlie felt a pang of guilt, scrambling for the comfort of a classic phrase generally held in high regard. Was it not always better to be safe than sorry?

"But what if we're safe and sorry?"

Two thousand light-years away, a small humanoid creature shuffled through a box of index cards, pulling a few out and glancing over them, and every time replacing them in the box.

He sighed, annoyed. He rifled through cards again.

"I guess 86 the imported cabbage salad," he said to his sous-chef in their native language, who took a dry-erase marker to a white board in their kitchen to notify the waitstaff that it would be unavailable. "We never received the cabbage of Earth."

He pulled another index card from the recipe box.

Gerald Beckman

Gerald Beckman was born and raised on a farm in West Texas, and has practiced law in Corpus Christi since 1969. Since retirement he has written five novels, two of which have been published, and two of which are presently in the hands of an agent. He continues to write, travel, and do all those things he always wanted to do but never had time for. He serves on numerous committees and boards, and enjoys volunteering in community activities such as World Affairs Council of South Texas, International Education Committee at TAMUCC, the Building Committee at St. John's Catholic Church, and Beautify Corpus Christi.

We Called it Baseball

Baseball as seen on television is the sport in its purest form. It's where a superman makes a perfectly timed jump against an outfield wall to snatch a fly ball over his back; where a third baseman dives for an 85 mph grounder, scoops it out of the dirt, rolls to his feet and in the same graceful motion shoots it like a rifle shot to first in time to make the out; where a pitcher throws a ball at 100 mph to a target 17 by 30 inches over sixty feet away, almost never hitting a man hunkered six inches away from the target, while making the ball curve and jump, hop, drop, or rise; where hulking batters who can swing a bat nearly as fast as the pitch face those brain-rattling fastballs zipping inches past their skulls without fear; where every player knows instantly and exactly what to do on the next play, no matter what it is, and does it time and time again, flawlessly. That is what people call baseball nowadays. That's what they talk about, that's what they analyze, and that's what they bet on while sitting in their living rooms sipping suds and nibbling nachos. It's baseball to be sure, but it's baseball in sanitized perfection. It's nothing like the baseball I once knew and loved.

I loved the nitty-gritty, the wild, untamed, unsponsored and unorganized, almost totally infertile spawning grounds for professional players that thrived before the disappearance of tiny country schools, before unlimited school sports budgets, manicured playing fields, and helicopter parenting; where kids discovered the game on their own, where they played without adult interference for the pure love of it, where money and fame and free-agenting and endorsements were as immaterial, albeit unattainable, as the back side of the moon; where coaching was nil, rules unknown, or misunderstood, often, even, not applicable, even in the unlikely event a rulebook could be found and the pertinent rule pinpointed. I loved that version of the game so much that, forty-five years later, I still dream of playing it.

I was in first grade when I first swung a bat at a slow pitched softball. I remember it to this day. The ball was tossed by some chubby girl in the fourth grade from what must have been every bit of ten feet away, and I couldn't hit it worth a flip. There was no backstop, no bleachers, no coaches, no organization, and no rules other than 1) try to hit the ball, and if you managed that, 2) run to first base, not third (a common mistake); 3) chase the ball (actually catching it was rare; even a slow grounder bouncing over the native pasture sod was harder to grab than a panicky ground squirrel); 4) throw the ball when you finally got to it, 5) run after it again, on and on until the bell rang at the end of recess.

Our equipment was one broken bat whose handle was repeatedly repaired by black electrical tape, and a ball whose cover kept coming off until some enterprising young lady had her mom stitch it back on. Rusty plow discs of different sizes placed at stepped-off distances forming a rough square served as bases, and a short piece of flat board placed somewhere close to the middle of the square was the pitcher's mound — except, of course, there was no mound. In the early grades boys and girls played the game together. Later we played boys against girls, and because we were stronger (loading hay bales all summer long) and faster (endlessly chasing livestock from one pasture to another), the boys usually won. But not always.

As we got older, we got more sophisticated. We chose teams, taking turns, starting with the best, ending with the worst. That was usually Joey Saren, a poor kid absolutely devoid of anything approaching physical grace, but who bore his repeated humiliations with a different kind of grace and no apparent psychic scars. No longer were the games played only at school, where we were limited to a fifteen minute recess at midmorning, a one hour lunch break—wolfing down our sack lunches in less than five minutes so we could play ball—and another fifteen minute recess at mid-afternoon. Now, with the freedom afforded by a few additional years and balloon-tired bicycles, we could play for hours at a time in some farmer's cow-pasture, using gunny sacks and flattened cardboard for bases. Still no coaching, bleachers or properly laid out diamond, but we did sometimes manage the side of a barn or storage shed as a backstop, and we had learned some of the rules, like a tie goes to the runner, a caught foul tip is a strike and not an out, and what a balk meant, though we could never agree exactly when it happened; and since the umpire was always the worst player (that's why he was umpire) and knew even less about the rules than the rest of us, he wasn't much help. It came down to which side shouted the loudest or was the readiest to quit if it didn't get its way.

Though these games lasted longer than the ones at school, they had a downside that made them less popular than they might have been. Dodging prickly pears and cow pies while chasing balls detracted considerably from the fun of the game.

I was fifteen when I took the next step up the ladder. I was accepted to play for the Umbarger Blue Socks, one of seven teams made up of farmers from my age on up (some guys were pushing fifty) who got together and organized themselves into what they called the West Texas Irrigation League.

We played every Sunday, each team taking its turn to host the game in the town closet to their farms. Never any practice sessions, no warmups, just show up and play. Still no coaching, no grandstands, no snack bars, and mostly worn-out equipment, except for our gloves. Every player had his own glove, a significant investment, and he kept it clean and oiled. One player named Billy Tubman (more about him later), on the theory that if a little bit of oil was good, a whole lot of oil was a whole lot better, soaked his glove in a bucket of motor oil overnight. Like the rest of us, he had no money to spare, so he did everything imaginable to undo the damage, including backing over it with a truck tire to squish the oil out of it, soaking it in a bucket of gasoline to dilute the oil, stuffing flour in and around it, hanging it from a tree limb to evaporate whatever would evaporate, and washing it over and over in hot water and detergent. He finally got it back to a useable condition, and years later, when I got married and quit the team, he was still using it. True story.

The hosting team would provide two new baseballs for that day's game, which we tried our best to make last. Young kids would race each other chasing the fouls, and if they returned it soon enough to use for the next pitch, we'd pay the winner a dime. Actually, we paid the dime anyway.

Our ball field was bounded on two sides by cow pastures, one along third base, the other beyond left and center fields. There was something about our games that attracted cows. They would start gathering along the fence toward the beginning of a game, and by the bottom of the ninth there were more cows watching than people. And since it's not easy to housebreak a cow, lots of manure piles were scattered about. Sometimes a foul ball rolled through a fresh pile, which was one of the fastest ways to age a new ball. We had a sackful of used balls for such occasions. We all agreed that if spitballs were illegal, shitballs ought to be illegal too. I don't remember who came up with that one, but everybody thought it was pretty funny.

But by then we did have a backstop. It was made of chickenwire mesh and cedar posts, and where the mesh overlapped, it was stitched together with baling wire. It didn't take long for gaps to develop, which were patched, and repatched, and repatched again, until finally a good portion of the backstop was nearly impossible to see through. It made little difference though, since there were so few spectators. Human ones, anyway.

The quality of play was pretty pathetic. Pathetic: how else describe hitting a slow grounder to the shortstop, the shortstop scooping it up to throw to first, overthrowing the first baseman, the ball bouncing off the bumper of a parked car, careening into a patch of pigweeds, the batter rounding first and heading for second while the first baseman looks frantically in the weeds for the ball, finds it, hurls it to third, which by now is the destination of the runner, who rounds third and heads for home while the third baseman, figuring on a sure out, grips the ball to throw home for the tag, only to learn the hard way that a goathead was stuck in the ball which is painfully transferred to his hand, causing another wild throw, all of which results in a home run?

How else describe the visiting team showing up only to discover it forgot its sack of bats, so we, ever the gentlemen, offer to share ours, until the home plate umpire, which they supplied, calls a strike on one of our guys when the pitch was so wild it went behind the batter, and later called another strike when the ball bounced six inches in front of the plate with enough speed and power to cover home plate in dust, which the ump duly swept off with his little brush, and in neither case would change his call, so when their time came to bat we repossessed our bats and forced a forfeit?

Or the time one of our players who had been in a month-long slump hit a solid line drive down the third base line which should have been an easy base hit, but, in an excess of elation, tossed his bat up in the air and when it came down hit his head, dropped to the ground in front of him causing him to trip and stumble, and while he's picking himself up, the left fielder throws the ball with all his might to first base, which doesn't quite make it, so the first baseman runs to pick it up, dashes back to first base just as the runner gets there, they crash head on, both collapse to the ground, the first baseman drops the ball and a huge argument ensues as to whether or not the runner is out. It was a complicated question: did the first baseman beat the runner or vice-versa? And what about the dropped ball? Was it dropped before the collision or after? The runner and the first baseman were in no mood to be toyed with and both had already been humiliated beyond tolerance, so the umpire, fearing for his life, refused to make the call. Some genius solved the problem and saved some broken noses in the process by suggesting a coin toss. I don't remember who won the toss, but everybody was satisfied.

And one more: How about the time during wheat harvest when everybody on the other side was busy cutting wheat (they were from a town a hundred miles south of Umbarger, so their harvest was in full swing and ours was just about to begin), and when their team showed up they were all girls! A high school girl team of fast-pitch softball players. Well, there were rules about who could or could not play on a West Texas Irrigation League team, one of which was, you had to be on the team's official roster for a certain amount of time, and none of these girls were on that roster for any amount of time.

And they were girls! Sweet innocent little high school girls. So what the hell, a sure win, right? Not exactly a macho thing to do, but the possibility of another mark in our win column trumped any notion of chivalry lurking in our black hearts, so yeah, okay, we'd waive the rules, hee-hee! We'd even let them pitch to us underhand. From forty feet away instead of sixty? Sure, why not? As long as our side could stick with the overhand style from sixty feet. Let's get it done and over with.

Who knew they were tenacious, single-minded, organized, coached, trained, talented, dedicated, determined, capable, fast, agile, coordinated, and for this game, particularly motivated? Ever try to hit a baseball thrown underhand at 70 miles an hour from forty feet away?

They beat our pants off.

We had only two pitchers, Sammy Nelson and Billy Tubman, he of oiled glove fame. Sammy was a tall, lanky kid, clumsy and slow as a milk cow, but had a fastball that could suck the whiskers off your chin. And he was wild; oh man, was he ever wild. We won more than one game because of the fear he instilled in at least half of all opposing batters. I can still see the pose of the terrified batters: absurdly open stance, gingerly crowding the left back corner of the batter's box, crouched, butt sticking over the edge of the box, front leg poised to collapse in a twisting plunge to the dirt, holding the bat at an impossible angle; what made it so fearsome was, the batter never knew whether a plunge toward the plate or away from it would give him the better chance. It's hard to hit a pitch from a stance like that, but those that did, and the ones brave enough to squelch their fears, were the ones that regularly beat us. Vengeance of a sort was ours though, because a good many of them went home with saucer-sized bruises on their hips and arms.

When he was on, Sammy would whizz the ball so straight down the center that the catcher didn't have to move his mitt a single centimeter to catch it. Sometimes he could do that several innings in a row, then something deep inside his control center would snap, and the walkathon would begin. A batter would be doing his jittery ready-to-dive dance at the corner of the batters' box, suffer through four or five, sometimes six pitches flying in his general direction, then, with great relief, trot off to first. Same with the next, and the next. Soon a slow, musical-chairs sort of shuffle was milling around the bases as one player after another took his place in the queue heading for home.

Five walks in a row wasn't unusual. That's two runs, assuming no one was on base when the first batter walked.

That's when Billy would take over.

Billy was a hulking bachelor who lived by himself on a farm about six miles west of town. His hands were the size of boxing gloves and his fingers the size of bratwurst sausages. His regular position was right field, but when he pitched, his specialty was the knuckler.

We all know that when you throw a ball, it spins, and if it spins fast enough in the right direction, it curves, rises, or drops. The reason is that the spin, in combination with the stitches, causes uneven air pressure on one side of the ball or the other. A good pitcher can control the spin so as to make it go up, down, or sideways.

But what if you throw the ball so it doesn't spin? When that happens, the air makes the ball wobble and the stitches to randomly change positions relative to the direction the ball moves through the air, with the result that it floats like, to quote Willie Stargell, a butterfly with hiccups. It's nearly impossible to hit. It's called a knuckle ball, or knuckler, and Billy, with his oversized hands, had the knuckle ball down pat. I always believed that if he had thrown the knuckle ball exclusively, we could have won every game we ever played.

But he wouldn't do it. He'd generally use it to strike out however many batters remained in the inning he relieved Sammy in, but then, no matter how much we badgered him, he'd revert to throwing what he considered his fast ball and his slow, sissy curve ball. Only problem was, his fastballs were as straight and pretty as the sunrise and not at all fast, and his curve balls had no more curves than a girl marathoner. That's why he never started. Nobody could persuade him to throw his knuckler if he didn't want to.

All that was the soup, the unitdy, unholy morass, the

confusing, confounding, and endlessly fascinating and mostly unproductive breeding grounds where on rare occasions, true genius nevertheless germinated, and on even rarer occasions came to fruition. I saw it happen. One of our players, a kid named Barry Sizemore, two years younger than I, joined our team when he was fifteen. We went to the same small country school (total number of students including grades one through 12, hovered around fifty. That's fifty, five-o, fifty), so I knew he was pretty good, but what the hell; he was just a skinny little twerp. He wouldn't jeopardize my team standing any.

Then in one season he must have added five inches to his height and twenty pounds of muscle to his frame. Long story short: he showed enough promise that his daddy sent him to a month-long baseball school somewhere in Oklahoma, and when he returned, not only did he dominate every game he played in, which was all of them, but scouts began showing up around the League's dilapidated facilities, not quite believing the five carat diamond they had found in the detritus. Whatever the rules were that governed professional recruiting, they prohibited scouts from even talking to Barry until he graduated high school, but when he walked off the stage on graduation night, he, under his daddy's wing, signed with one of the majors. I think it was Brooklyn. Later that summer Brooklyn played a demonstration game in Phoenix, and the first time at bat, Barry hit one out of the park.

His mistake was marrying the wrong girl. She didn't like him gone all the time, so he quit baseball after one year, bought a farm with his bonus money, fathered eight children, lost the farm, divorced his wife, remarried, and now lives in some small West Texas town pumping gas and bemoaning his lost chance. And what a chance it was. He was a natural. The only coaching he ever got, from anybody, was during the month he spent in Oklahoma, where he beat Mickey Mantle's record for time from home plate to first base. True story.

That's the baseball I remember and love. Is today's version of the game better? Undoubtedly.

But it's not as much fun.

Kenneth Bennight

Kenneth Bennight is a husband, father, lawyer, former Marine, and native Texan, and the grandfather of the cutest little boy on the face of the Earth. Kenneth grew up in Corpus Christi and graduated from Ray High School. He now resides in San Antonio, Texas, and is the author of the hard-boiled Nacho Perez stories, Nacho Perez, Private Eye and The Truth Shall Make You Dead. Those stories and others are available on Amazon.

Found Money

Where the hell was the damn center stripe? Thad Will peered ahead. The wipers and the full-blast defroster kept only a patch of the windshield clear from freezing rain. His headlights barely penetrated the blur. He kept his speed around 40 miles per hour, his knuckles aching from his tight grip on the wheel. When was the last time South Texas had weather like this? His eyelids felt heavy.

He blinked and rubbed his eyes. No sleep in almost two days. Getting a room in Cotulla would have been good. If he could afford it. But Eagle Ford work had slowed and threatened to disappear. He couldn't spend money on motels with Justin needing braces and the dining room set about to be repossessed.

His eyes closed, his body relaxed, he almost slid into sleep, and the car started to drift. Adrenalin hit. His eyes popped back open, and he jerked the car straight. Damn it all. He repeatedly slapped his cheek.

He hadn't seen another car since leaving Cotulla, shortly before he'd passed a sign warning that the next gas station was 94 miles down the road. FM 624 cuts east-west across the South Texas brush. He'd heard it called the world's longest hunting lease. Traffic was seldom heavy, and only an idiot would travel it on a night like this.

Headlights reflected in his rear-view mirror. Who else was out in this mess? A few seconds later, he realized the lights were approaching fast. Jeez. Whoever this schmuck was, he was blasting along, ice be damned.

Moments later a new Ford Mustang swung wide around him and careened back, nearly clipping his front end. It swerved and slid down the road for as far as he could see. A nutso with a death wish. Will held his speed down.

Ten minutes later, he saw headlights ahead and to the side of the road. Maybe there's a curve. He studied the lights as he drew nearer. Something wasn't right.

Just a hundred yards short of the lights, he caught sight of a bridge. Ice. Shit. He thumped his brakes just before he crossed onto it and slid almost to the guard rail before regaining control.

Beyond the bridge, the Mustang lay spun around and upside down against the fence. He pulled over, turned on his flashers, and took a flashlight from his glove box. His feet crunched on the icy grass, which brushed against his ankles above his low-quarter shoes. Moisture wicked up his socks, leaving his feet wet and nearly numb.

The spider-web cracks in the window glass kept him from seeing inside. He wrestled open the driver's door, which cut an arced swath in the icy grass. A fruity, pungent alcohol smell slapped him in the face.

A sprawled body, feet to the front and head to the rear. The latter lay at an odd angle. No pulse. This fool had been driving like a madman without a seatbelt. A broken bottle of Jose Cuervo lay next to the driver.

He shone the light around to look for a passenger. No one. He was about to return to his car and call in the accident when he glimpsed something mostly obscured by the driver's body. He kneeled in the grass, and shone the light inside. Please God, don't let it be a child.

It was a duffel bag, the zipper slightly open – with a bundle of money sticking out. He pulled, but the driver's body held it down. When the bag finally came free, the driver's torso partly followed the bag out the door. Ice trickled down the back of Will's neck. His wet hair lay plastered against his head. He shook himself, caught his breath, and unzipped the bag all the way.

The bag was full of bundled hundred-dollar bills. His jaw dropped. Were they real? He glanced at the slumped body. Who was this guy? A drug dealer. Had to be.

He pulled out his cellphone to call the police but then stopped. Rain and melting ice soaked his clothes. He climbed to his feet and looked up and down the highway. Nobody had passed and still no cars in sight. He stuffed the body back in the car and closed the door as best he could, but the latch wouldn't catch. He locked the bag in his trunk and headed down the highway, setting the car's heater on high.

The right thing was to turn the money in. But if he did, they'd know he'd been at the accident and didn't report it immediately, and they'd know he'd tampered with a crime scene. Shit. He shook his head. I should go back. He took his foot off the accelerator. Then he thought of his debts. He needed that money. He sped back up.

He kept wrestling with the dilemma. He pulled over, shut off the engine, and turned on his flashers. The money wasn't his. He couldn't keep it. He leaned his head against the steering wheel and squeezed his eyes shut.

It had to be drug money. He took a deep breath. The druggies play for high stakes. Might even be cartel. What if they found him? Then I'm dead. It wasn't worth it. He should go back.

He reached for the ignition. But they weren't going to find him. Nobody saw anything. For all the druggies knew, the driver could have stashed the money somewhere else before he crashed.

He had to clear his mind. He slumped and focused on breathing regularly.

Tap, tap, tap.

He awoke, shivering. Flashing lights showed in the rearview mirror, and a patrolman stood at his window. He turned the key so he could lower his window. The rain and ice had let up.

"Is everything all right, sir?" The patrolman was tall and haggard, and his right hand rested on the butt of his pistol. He gave no sign the cold bothered him. The name tag on his chest read Corcoran.

"Yes, officer. Everything's fine. I just got a little sleepy, so I pulled over to doze. The cold's got me awake now." Will shifted in his seat and ran his fingers through his hair.

Corcoran moved his flashlight beam around the interior of Will's car. "Show me your license and insurance."

Will pulled his license out of his wallet, handed it over, and fumbled in his glove box until he came up with the insurance card. Thank God he'd kept up the payments.

Corcoran took the papers and went back to his patrol car. When he came back, he returned the papers. "Where're you headed?"

"Corpus Christi."

Corcoran looked him and his car over again. "You're soaked. Did you have some trouble back there?"

Will's mind raced.

"Uh, no, not really." He gulped. "The car, uh, well, it felt funny, and I thought maybe, uh, maybe I had a flat." The last words came more quickly than the previous ones, and he continued almost glibly. "I got out to check it, but the tire was fine." He offered Corcoran his most innocent smile.

"Pretty wet for just that."

Will shrugged. "I guess it took me a bit."

"I see." Corcoran raised his eyebrows and glared at Will as if he didn't see at all.

Will struggled not to wither. "May I leave now?"

Corcoran nodded. "Be careful, sir. It's a messy night. My radio said there's a bad wreck back nearer Cotulla."

Will bit his lower lip. "I hope the driver's OK."

Corcoran looked into his eyes. "I didn't say there was just one car or just one person in it."

"I guess I just assumed." Inspiration hit. "Were more people involved?"

"The officer on the scene said someone had been there. You know anything about that?"

Wills shook his head repeatedly. "No, sir. I don't, no. Not about that." Despite the cold, perspiration formed on Will's upper lip.

Corcoran stared but waved him on.

Will made a point of signaling to return to the traffic lane and headed east.

That settled that. He couldn't go back. They'd found the wreck, and they had a record of his whereabouts. He kept driving.

He slammed the steering wheel and grinned. Hell, he'd spend the money. Pay off bills, buy a new car, a new TV. Megan wanted to remodel the kitchen. He could just deposit the cash and start writing checks.

But what if the IRS audited him? No way could he explain the deposit. He shook his head. A lot of shit to think about. He'd ask Harry. Hypothetical, like. Harry worked for H&R Block during tax season. He'd know.

Another thought came to mind. He'd seen enough movies to know the druggies put GPS trackers in with their money. Less than two hours after his encounter with the patrolman, he pulled into the lot of the Stripes truck stop in Orange Grove, the only place open in the wee hours of a Sunday morning. He parked under a flood light at the back of the empty lot, retrieved the duffel from the trunk, and got back in the car to open it. The bundles all seemed to be the same size, and the bills were all Franklins, one-hundred dollars. He counted one bundle out. One hundred Franklins. Ten grand in a bundle. He found seventy-five bundles. Seven hundred fifty grand. A life-changing sum.

In the bottom sure enough his fingers found the tracker. He pulled it out and held it to the light. Were they already on his trail? Was he already a dead man? He looked around. Nothing, nobody. He had to get rid of it fast. He took several deep breaths. Don't be paranoid.

A big rig pulled into the lot. The driver left the engine idling and went inside the store. Inspiration hit Will. He could stick the gizmo on the truck. But it didn't look waterproof. He looked at the sky. If he didn't keep it dry, he might as well throw it in a dumpster.

He returned the bag with the money to his trunk, keeping the GPS, and followed the driver inside. Rancid oil from the popcorn machine permeated the room. Microwaveable sandwiches and burritos lay at one end of the store and the counter lay at the other. In between were rows of candy, cookies, chips, toiletries, and cans of oil and radiator coolant.

The truck driver headed to the restroom. Will laid a Coke and a chocolate candy bar on the counter and, after they were scanned, slid his credit card through the reader. Coke and chocolate would both give him much needed caffeine.

"You need a bag for that?" the clerk asked.

"Yes, please."

Back at his car, he put the gizmo in the Stripes' plastic bag and used duct tape from his trunk to secure the bag to the locking bar on the back of the idling big-rig's trailer. Then he waited. The driver returned to his rig, pulled out of the Stripes, and headed north toward Mathis. Hallelujah.

Will headed east to Corpus. When he got home in the wee hours of the morning, he stuffed the bag in the back of a closet and crawled into bed next to Megan. He lay awake for an hour, maybe two.

The next morning, over coffee, he brooded. He considered depositing some of the cash at an ATM and remembered to call Harry.

Harry chuckled. "You win the lottery, pal? You know they're going to report that anyway."

Will ground his teeth. "No, nothing like that. You know, a friend and I at work had a bet about how to do this."

"A bet with a friend is an old one, buddy, You must have knocked over a drug dealer."

"Up yours." Will hung up the phone.

Will Googled large cash deposits and found a bewildering array of rules requiring currency transaction reports and cash-transaction records, some for transactions as low as $3,000. Screw that. He'd keep the cash.

He wasn't due back in Cotulla until Wednesday. On Monday, he paid off the dining room set and prepaid the orthodontist for Justin's braces. That evening, after Justin was in bed, he called Megan over to the table and laid out the receipts and the bag with the money.

Her weary eyes turned quizzical as she flipped through the receipts. "What's this?"

"I paid for Justin's braces and paid off the balance on the furniture."

She poked in the bag and gasped.

"Where did you get this?" She paused and looked into his eyes. "Thad, what have you done?" Her voice was soft and higher pitched than normal.

He told her about the wrecked car and the duffel bag. He left out the highway patrolman and the GPS tracker.

Megan ran a hand through her hair. "You've got to give it

back. It's not ours."

"Well . . . ." He explained about Officer Corcoran.

She shook her head. "You've made a mess."

He took her hand. "Only if you look at it that way. Look at it as a gift."

Tuesday morning, Will read the neighborhood crime blotter and looked up at Megan.

"Did you read about these burglaries? Somebody might steal the money."

Megan tilted her head and looked at him sideways. "Irony's not your long suit, is it?"

He waved her off. He needed to spread the risk of losing the money, keep some of it somewhere else. He stuffed $400,000 into his attic crawl space. He took the unspent remainder in the original duffel bag to the rented storage space where they stored stuff they should have gotten rid of.

* * *

Monday afternoon after Will's early Sunday morning trek through Orange Grove, Laurencio Contreras sat in the Stripes parking lot. The sun was out, and the temperature had risen to the mid-60s. Texas weather.

El Jefe had been pissed when the GPS took the wrong path. Laurencio caught up with the driver at a Victoria truck stop, and when he was done with him, Laurencio believed the guy knew nothing. But Laurencio had to find the cash fast if he wanted to stay on el Jefe's good side. He didn't want to see el Jefe's bad side.

He'd traced the GPS's movements. It had stopped three times before Victoria. The bag must have been taken at the first stop, where the mule had wrecked. The pinche borracho.

Laurencio didn't understand the second stop on an isolated stretch of road, but the Stripes had to be where the GPS got on the truck. He surveyed the lot and spotted surveillance cameras.

Inside the store, his nose wrinkled at the rancid-oil smell. He browsed the merchandise and picked up a Big Red and an Almond Joy. Just below another surveillance camera, a picture of the manager hung on the wall, conveniently labeled with a name, Buddy Jaramillo. But someone other than Buddy stood behind the register.

When Laurencio stepped up to the counter, he set down his purchases and pointed at the picture. "I think I went to school with that vato. Is he here today?"

"Naw, he's off."

"Live nearby?" Laurencio added a Snickers bar to his purchase.

"Yeah, last house on the left on West Josephine."

At the last house on West Josephine, a boy practiced dribbling and tried to make baskets in a hoop without a net. A scraggly mesquite grew at the corner of the driveway. Laurencio turned his car to face back the way he'd come and called out.

"Oye. are you Buddy's boy?"

The boy got control of his ball and held it as his side. "Yes, sir." He brushed aside his dark hair from his forehead.

"Is your daddy home?"

"He went to the grocery store, but he'll be back soon."

"I'll wait for him." Laurencio stepped out of the car but left his engine running. He held the candy bar out. "Would you like this?"

"Sure." The boy approached, and Laurencio grabbed him, one hand over the boy's mouth. The boy struggled and tried to scream, but Laurencio stuffed him in the back seat.

"When I let go of your mouth, you make noise, I twist your head until your neck snaps. You got me?" The boy nodded, tears gushing down his cheeks. Slowly, Laurencio released the boy's mouth. The boy sobbed but made no other noise. Laurencio gagged him and used two zip ties, one to bind his hands and another his feet.

He drove back down FM 624 until he found several rows of large, round hay bales lying near the road. He cut the fence, dumped the boy between rows, and left him among piles of dried cow manure.

When Laurencio got back to the house, a large man stood in the front yard shouting, "Jesse. Jesse. Get back home, boy." The man matched the picture of Buddy Jaramillo.

Laurencio turned his car back around again, got out, and lifted his shirt tail to reveal a gun. "You want to see your boy again? Do what I say. Comprende?"

Buddy's eyes raced back and forth between the gun and Laurencio's face. "What have you done to my boy? Where is he?"

Laurencio touched his gun. "Get in the driver's seat. We're going to the Stripes. Show me video from two nights ago. Then, you see your boy."

Almost as many tears ran down Buddy's face as had his son's. "You didn't have to take my boy for this."

"Just do it."

At the Stripes, Buddy waited until the clerk finished with a customer and then beckoned.

"We're going to be in the office. Leave us undisturbed."

The clerk nodded.

In the small office in the back of the Stripes, Buddy and Laurencio pulled up the video. Running through it was excruciating, even at twice the normal speed. The later the hour, the longer between customers. After a long period of inactivity, a car pulled in and parked under a light. Laurencio recognized the duffel the driver took from the trunk. When the driver went into the store, Laurencio had Buddy load the interior video. When he saw the credit card transaction, Laurencio's grin turned cold, and he had Buddy pull up the buyer's name and credit card number.

Armed with a name, Laurencio called el Jefe. Then he turned to Buddy and pointed.

"That way up 624, in some hay bales." He grabbed Buddy's forearm, boring his eyes into Buddy's. "You say anything about this to anyone, I know where you live. Anything. Claro?"

"Sí, claro." Buddy gulped air. "I got you."

When Laurencio returned to his car and reached for the ignition, el Jefe called with an address to match the name. Laurencio headed for Corpus. He found Will's house and spent the night in his car down the block where he had a good view. Cars littered the curb, so Laurencio's didn't stand out. He chuckled when Will left Tuesday morning with the duffel. Pinche gringo. Mueres pronto.

* * *

The Sunday afternoon after his early-morning encounter with Thad Will, Earl Corcoran propped up his feet on the coffee table and took a puff on his cigar. Marisol never would have let him put his feet on the table—or smoke a cigar in the house. But when he'd gotten home, all he found was a spite letter calling him a low-life. She'd packed up the kids and headed for her parents. At the beginning of his week off. Bitch.

He shook his head. Dwelling on Marisol's letter wasn't a good idea. His mind turned to the squirrel last night on 624. Will had been at the wreck. His nervousness, his being soaked, and his comments about the wreck. All that clinched it. Will had to be the one.

He chugged the rest of his beer. A week without family. Hell. He might as well stake the bastard out.

Tuesday morning, Corcoran watched Will leave the house with a duffel bag. A blue-shirted Hispanic male in a car down the street followed Will. Corcoran followed them both.

Will traveled down South Padre Island Drive until he pulled into a sun-and-salt-bleached storage facility. It consisted of five wings of storage rooms all running perpendicular to a once-white office in the front. Will entered a code and went through an automatic gate. Blue Shirt's car squeezed through and paused by a nearby storage unit. Corcoran grimaced, taking Blue Shirt's pause as an effort to lull Will.

Corcoran ran through the office, holding out his badge to a sleepy clerk, who had incense burning. From the back door, Corcoran looked down one of the rows. Someone with a pickup was loading a mattress and box springs. Will's car came into view as it passed to the right along a cross drive. Corcoran turned to the right just as he caught a glimpse of Blue Shirt's car.

When Corcoran got to the next opening, he saw Will traveling away from him down the row. Will stopped, unlocked a unit, and took the duffel from his car. Blue Shirt whipped around a corner and skidded toward Will. He hopped out of his car and popped off a round in Will's direction.

"Give me the bag, pendejo, and maybe I'll let you live." Will tossed the duffel into view.

Corcoran aimed his Glock at Blue Shirt and called out, "DPS. Drop your weapon."

Blue Shirt wheeled and fired at the new target. Corcoran flinched when he felt the whoosh of the slug flying by his ear. Corcoran aimed center of mass and let off two rounds, but Blue

Shirt was moving. The shots missed.

Will scuttled around the next corner and peeked back at the fight. Blue Shirt took aim and fired at Corcoran. At the same instant, Corcoran fired back.

Corcoran grabbed his side. Damn. Pain spread across his upper body. Blue Shirt's round had probably broken a rib, but Blue Shirt had dropped from view. *At least I got the bastard.*

He approached where he'd last seen Blue Shirt. Not there. The opened storage unit. Corcoran stepped toward it, but a round slammed into his back. Corcoran staggered and fell to his knees. Blue Shirt had hidden behind Will's car.

Blue Shirt staggered to where he had a clear line of fire at Corcoran and fired three rounds, all of which connected. Corcoran got off two rounds and stayed conscious long enough to see Blue Shirt collapse in a pool of blood.

* * *

Will winced at the sirens. He looked longingly at the duffel, but fear paralyzed him. The first officer arrived in moments and others soon followed. Two dead men and a bag full of money greeted them. Will needed a story. Fast.

"I was just checking my storage unit, you know, to see if it was OK. I hadn't been here in a while. Then these two guys started shooting at each other. I nearly got hit, but I hid around the corner. I don't know what it was about."

Will wasn't sure the cops believed him, but they let him go after a few hours. The evening news gave him hope.

> Off-duty DPS Officer Earl Corcoran was killed today in a gunfight with known drug trafficker Laurencio Contreras, who also died in the encounter. Police recovered a large sum of money at the scene, money that will be forfeited as presumed proceeds of the drug trade. A police spokesman said this was a major blow against a cartel run by a man known as El Jefe.

The story didn't say how much money was in the bag. The bad guys would think the cops had it all. Will thought of the

$400,000 in his attic. Only Megan and he knew.

* * *

Buddy Jaramillo's jerked up straight in his chair. The slain drug trafficker shown on TV was the guy who kidnapped Jesse and watched the security tapes. Then the reporter mentioned a Thad Wills. That was the name on the credit card receipt. Buddy reached for the phone and called the sheriff.

Alan Berecka

Alan Berecka was named the Poet Laureate of Corpus Christi in February 2017. His latest collection, The Hamlet of Stittville, is a collaboration with the New Yorker cartoonist and boyhood friend John Klossner. Berecka earns his keep as a reference librarian at Del Mar College. His work has appeared in such publications as Red River Review, Texas Review, The Christian Century, Windhover, Ruminate, St. Peter's B-List and Oklahoma Poems...And Their Poets.

Commuting

How far can a fog lift
before it becomes a cloud?

Whatever it was, it hung
above the causeway,
a few feet above each car
and truck, as we drove
over the shallow end
of the Gulf, consumed
with the needs
of our daily commute.

I noticed how the gulls
and pelicans disappeared
diving up into the thickness
but thought little of it, until
I rounded the long curve
near the final exit,
and there it hung
like a shroud, completely
obscuring the upper two-thirds
of the Harbor Bridge.

While being pulled along

by the constant traffic,
I watched the countless
sets of tail lights
ascending into obscurity,
taking on faith that beyond
it still lies the bridge
into the city of Corpus Christi.

Cynthia Breeding

Cynthia Breeding often wonders if she was born in the wrong century. She has a love/hate relationship with technology and has an avid interest in medieval history. Most of her books are historical romances with a bit of paranormal thrown in now and then. She also loves sailing and horseback riding. Cynthia is a well-established romance writer with 49 novels and novellas available.

Excerpt from **Bedroom Blarney**

Chapter One

"Vodka martini, extra dry. Two olives."

"Yes, Ma'am. Coming right up."

As the bartender moved away to get her drink, Eve O'Connor closed her wet umbrella and plopped it alongside her satchel on the empty barstool next to her and pinched the bridge of her nose to relieve tension. TGIF had never sounded so good. Her art classes had been crap today. Not one high school kid had taken notes on value and hue in color and they certainly had not cared about line and space in composition.

Given the array of video games on smart phones and tablets, it was getting harder to get her students interested—let alone keep them interested—in something as mundane as classical art. Little wonder newbie teachers lasted less than two years in many cases. She had even contemplated changing careers herself, but Joe, her worthless ex-husband, had gambled away her savings before she'd caught him and she was still paying off the cost of the divorce. Besides, she had almost ten years invested in Deer Hill High School.

"Why so glum?" a male voice asked behind her. "It is Friday, after all."

Eve turned to find her friend, Chad Olson, grinning at her as he pulled out the stool on her other side. Adonis good-looking, with sun-streaked blond hair and nearly cobalt-colored eyes, the few women in the bar this early were already eyeing him. Combined with his athletic football-coach build, Eve suspected they wouldn't be alone for long before one of the ladies sent over a drink.

"I'm just tired," she said as the bartender placed the martini in front of her and automatically started her tab. "Rough week."

"I hear you. Reynolds sprained an ankle in practice yesterday and the game with O.U. is tomorrow."

"Your starting quarterback?" The only reason Eve followed college football was because Chad was a coach for Dallas-Fort Worth Metro University. "What will you do? I thought that game was supposed to be close."

"It is. Sims is going to have to fill in. Makes me glad I'm not the head coach though. If we lose, he's going to take a lot of heat." Chad's phone beeped, alerting him he had a Blog Face message. His face turned dark as he read it. "Damn it."

"Problem?"

"Just my wife wanting to know when I'll be home." He slipped the phone back into his pocket without replying and took a big swig of the beer the bartender had brought. "I'm getting sick of being nagged."

Eve nibbled on one of the olives at the end of her toothpick and glanced over. "Angelina probably just wants some adult company."

"If I believed that, maybe I'd go home. All she does is dote on the kid though."

"Why don't you get a sitter and go out to dinner? Make it a romantic evening."

Chad grimaced. "The last time we tried that, she kept calling home every ten minutes. For Christ's sake, Jessica is almost two."

At least, Eve didn't have that problem. Joe hadn't been inclined toward fatherhood and maybe Fate had smiled on her that she hadn't gotten pregnant. And, at thirty-two, she didn't feel an urge for single motherhood either. Children were cute, as long as they were someone else's.

The bartender set another beer down in front of Chad and inclined his head. "From the brunette over there."

"Thanks." Chad turned and smiled at the woman, lifting the stein in salute. She inhaled, lifting half-exposed breasts and smiled back. He turned back to Eve. "Looks like a score. Maybe I should cancel my other appointment."

"Other appointment?"

Chad tapped the phone in his shirt pocket. "Met a girl on Blog Face last week."

"How many does that make?"

"A few." He shrugged. "Less than ten anyway. I don't keep them around long enough for anyone to dig her claws into me."

Eve motioned to the bartender for another martini. "Just a thought, but I don't suppose you mention you're married?"

"Why should I? I'm just getting a little action. I don't lead anyone on." He looked at the brunette and winked. She winked back. "You see?" he said to Eve, "it's an open invitation. Why turn it down?"

"Well, Angelina is waiting. Besides, the brunette hardly looks old enough to be legal." She knew that sounded snide, but she couldn't help herself.

Chad frowned. "What's gotten into you? You're seeing Caldwell—my married boss—so it's not exactly like you're wearing a halo."

"That's different."

He arched a brow. "Really? How so?"

Eve sipped her martini before answering. "I knew Brian was married. He was upfront about it."

"A fact he could hardly hide, since you met his wife at the same party."

"True, but his kids are older and Brenda is involved with so many charities, she's hardly ever home. It's not like I'm interfering with their marriage."

His eyebrow rose higher. "Did you discuss it with her?"

Eve felt her cheeks warm. "Of course not. The point is, I am not looking for commitment or another husband, so she has nothing to worry about. I like having sex though. Is that so wrong? A married lover is very safe. Neither of us has expectations beyond a good time in bed."

"I'll agree with you there," Chad said and set his empty mug down. "And, if you'll excuse me, I think I'll go see about showing that little brunette over there a very good time."

Brandon Cantu/Melinda Cantu

Brandon Cantu was given a school assignment in creative writing when he was 6 years old. He and his mother, Melinda Cantu, chose to use a porcupine as subject material based on a TV documentary they had seen.

Quillan Control Your Temper!

This is a story about a porcupine named Quillan. Quillan was a very nice porcupine except he had one big problem. Quillan could not control his temper.

Every day he would play baseball with his friends. When it was his turn to bat if the pitcher would strike him out he would get so MAD! Quillan would arch his back, tighten his muscles and his quills would stand straight up. His friends were so afraid to get close to him for fear of being stuck with one of his quills that they would all run away.

This made Quillan very sad. He went home and told his Mom, "No one wants to play with me." His Mom said, "Quillan you have to CONTROL YOUR TEMPER!" "But Mom how do I control my temper?" Quillan asked. She said, "Try counting to ten."

So the next day he went out to play baseball as usual. It was his turn to bat. "Strike Three! You're out!" yelled the umpire. Quillan could feel himself getting angry. His back started to arch, his muscles started to tense up. "One, two, three, four…" But it was no use. By that time his quills were sticking straight up and everyone ran away.

Quillan went home very sad. "Mom, I tried counting to ten but it did not work" he said. His Mom said, "Quillan you have to CONTROL YOUR TEMPER! Try taking deep breaths."

So the next day he went out to play baseball as usual. It was his turn to bat. "Strike Three! You're out!" yelled the umpire. Quillan could feel himself getting angry. His back started to arch, his muscles started to tense up. "Hum, Whew, Hum, Whew…" But it was no use. By that time his quills were sticking straight up and everyone ran away.

Quillan was so sad. "Mom it didn't work." His Mom said, "Quillan you have to CONTROL YOUR TEMPER! Try walking away".

So the next day he went out to play baseball as usual. It was his turn to bat. "Strike Three! You're out!" yelled the umpire. Quillan could feel himself getting angry. His back started to arch, his muscles started to tense up. Quillan tried walking away. But by that time everyone had run away. POOR QUILLAN!

Quillan was very sad. That night he thought about his problem and came up with an idea.

The next day he went out to play baseball as usual. It was his turn to bat. "Strike Three! You're out!" yelled the umpire. Quillan started counting to ten, "One, two, three, four" . . . then he started taking deep breaths, "Hum, Whew, Hum, Whew". . . then he walked away from home plate. Guess what! It worked!

Quillan learned how to CONTROL HIS TEMPER. Everyone was so proud of him. "Hooray for Quillan!" everyone yelled.

Quillan was so proud of himself also because that day not only did he learn to control his temper but he even got to hit a homerun.

Robin Carstensen

Robin Carstensen was a medic and Orthopedic Surgery technician in the Air Force. Now she directs the creative writing program at TAMUCC where she teaches and advises The Windward Review, a literary journal of Texas Coastal Bend, and is co-founding, senior editor of the Switchgrass Review: literary journal of health and transformation focusing on women and lgbtq. Her first-place chapbook-winner, In theTemple of Shining Mercy, was published by Iron Horse Literary Press in 2017.

Breaking Point

Beyond the Buena Vida Senior Village
sprawled across the old grain field,
your cloud nearly touches his hovering
over the desk, where you've both made it
after all to this last office down the hall,
far end of Del Mar West, the outreach campus —
edge of the oil refinery city, South Texas
Gulf Coast, where you finally finished
your own heavy lifting, defended
your dissertation after playing medic,
dishwasher, short-order cook, pizza-hut
deliverer, now trying to catch a new
break, he lifts his draft — essay one —
above the shaft of afternoon dust,
gauzy thick like revision-talk for making
clear and academically sound his life
on the industrial edge, the drug lords
who track him to every address,
tempt him with rolls of bills — favor
for his father and brother behind
Beeville's bars, whose sealed mouths
and flared eyes command him to stay

his course. The vapor from their locked-in
dreams beating like the Royal Tern's
wings heavy with metal residue
lifting against the chemical sky
has gathered in the atmosphere
of his face and yours when you look
into the large, black shades that veil
his eyes, you freeze, hear the distant
pierce of an engine's gullet full-throttling
down Old Brownsville Road, or urgent
call of gull. The sound is closing in,
and now it strikes you — here, escaping
his throat. His brick shoulders shake,
his lips are wet, and the issue at stake
is cracking the surface, beyond the point
of saturation, his life, and yours, dark
chambers in the cold room about to break.

Ghazal: Reclamation

No one taught us how to reach without burning. We were playing house and healing
    our inner child, without the tidy scripts for moral resolution. We were wounds of healing.

I was, you were bereft. When love leaves the beloved who was flame whole, or is left,
    how the skin shifts, each organ a dune. Or become stone. Can a stone find healing?

Someone stole my rose bush in its plastic pot. I found it on a neighbor's porch, strained
    my neurons for a way to reclaim it without war. It bloomed into my neighbor's healer.

I wanted a fairy godmother. I wanted a peach cobbler. I want to stop chasing the holy
    mother grail, like the bird in Dr. Seuss's "Are You My Mother?" My long lost healer?

I am still torn between feeling enlightened — *for every atom belonging to me as good*
    belongs to you — and feeling like a coward for not defending my rose bush, my healing.

I was supposed to be your goddess, and you mine. I can't go to Nirvana, for the life
    of me. Your splintered heart is a blue medallion shaped like feathers, song, healing.

I didn't ask for the rose bush back, and he didn't give it back. Sometimes nobody
    gives anything back or says sorry, and you're a divining rod of your own healing.

    I had a job turning a man on his hospice bed to prevent decubitus ulcers. One night
        drunk, he drove across the divide. He became paralyzed, neck down. What healing

        could help him let that go? We were all different stories of letting go and grasping,
            thinking myth and romance and surely someone to catch us, some god, some Healer.

        When I turned his body in my arms toward me, we snapped our breaths back, our wild
            branches gripping winter wind, snow falling and freezing everything dormant, healing.

William Basileios Chriss, J.D, Ph.D.

Dr. Bill Chriss is a trial and appellate lawyer who is also a historian, political scientist, religious scholar, and published author. He was nominated for the Rhodes Scholarship and holds graduate degrees in law, theology, history and politics, including a J.D. from Harvard and a Ph.D. in history from The University of Texas. Dr. Chriss has taught Political Philosophy, History, and Constitutional Law and has written several articles for scholarly journals. His first book, The Noble Lawyer, was published by Texas Bar Books in 2011, while his second book, Six Constitutions over Texas, is currently being edited for publication.

Sirens

I can't sleep. Sirens whine and pulses of light flash red on the walls of this dingy hotel. There are only ten channels on the television and no wifi, and I'm stuck another night. All the flights home had departed by the time those New York lawyers finished interrogating the witness. Their hourly rates are higher than mine; certainly their cost of living is, so I understand. It's a long time since our firm, too, had more than enough work, a long time since the days when practicing law was an adventure and billings were mere bookkeepers' annoyances. I remember trying ten or fifteen cases a year with files only two inches thick – comp cases, fender benders, divorces, DWIs, and occasionally the more complex civil case or white-collar crime.

But maybe more than the law practice has been transformed. Maybe I was different then, too. Maybe I'm just growing old, inexorable change befuddling my calcifying brain. Maybe everything was wrong. Maybe I just took the wrong path. Maybe I'll never rest, never feel that I can go up to my house justified, never, like the prodigal son, come to myself and return where I belong. Maybe that place where I belonged is gone.

This kind of racing inner monologue keeps me awake more and more these days. The last in a long string of failed relationships ended two years ago when Jennifer stopped taking my calls or acknowledging my texts. We started out well enough, but like several before her, she eventually came to pity my failure to conquer the world. I used to be afraid to die alone. Now living, and even dying, alone is the only liberation I know of or hope for. I have grown used to the idea. I pronounce it good. What choice do I have? I'm tired of being hurt.

I must finally have dozed off. Awakening to find a grey dawn peeking through the curtains, I figure my partners won't begrudge me a long trip back. And maybe the client won't flyspeck the travel time charged for this deposition on the next invoice. I should be able to drop by the museum before heading to the airport and still get back to North Padre by dark. I'm not crazy about museums, but Michael told me of a painting here. In my current state of mind, any suggestion might bring an epiphany, so I shower, shave, and set out into the icy morning.

The museum down the street is small and old. Most of the art is uninteresting. "Where is the painting of Odysseus?" I ask an usher in a silly red coat.

"In the next gallery to the left."

And there indeed it is, surrounded by a heavy wood frame with a small brass plaque reading: "Odysseus and the Sirens by Herbert James Draper, 1909." I am struck by the image of Odysseus tied to the mast of his ship, straining against the ropes, head thrust forward in anguished longing for the evanescent female beings flitting along the rails of the boat. They are singing, chanting, moaning, songs of home.

"It speaks to one, does it not?" The accented voice startles me from behind. French? Austrian? I turn to see its owner, a bearded man in oddly formal attire.

"I guess," I mutter.

"Yes, well, I would judge that you are old enough to have been taught such stories in school before they were deemed irrelevant. It must have been quite a test for poor Odysseus, don't you think? Ten years of war at Troy; ten years of wandering after; cursed by the gods; far from home; captured by the Cyclops; seduced and enchanted by Circe and Calypso; drugged by the lotus eaters; and yet somehow never losing the desire to return home... home to his long suffering wife Penelope. And so when he entered the waters inhabited by these lovely nude creatures, as Draper depicts them, isn't it strange that he did what he did?"

"I don't know," I answer, "And I'm not sure there ever was a Penelope, then or now."

"Yes, but think on this part of the story. Odysseus knew the siren song was irresistible, that ...ah...it had lured all the ships before him onto the rocks, and so he tells his men to fill their ears with wax and to row for their lives no matter what they see. But here is the interesting part: he needs to hear the song himself; ah...he accords to himself the privilege of hearing the song, and so he does not plug his own ears. Instead he has the men tie him to the mast so he can do nothing to stop the progress of the ship. He is the hero, the adventurer, but he is also the wise man. He thinks ahead to protect the crew...and himself...from his need for mystical experience. Without the wisdom, the experience will ruin him; he will never get home."

"Whatever that might mean."

"Yes," the old man says, "whatever that might mean, and I suppose it acquires a more difficult meaning when one gets to be Odysseus's age, about the same age as Hemingway when he died, and, I would think, perhaps about the same age as you."

I turn my attention back to the painting. Odysseus' eyes are agape, almost crazy. The sirens appear pale, ghostlike, mesmerizing. They hover close to Odysseus's oarsmen, who are looking directly at them without expression, apparently oblivious. Is the crew blind as well as deaf? Or are the sirens somehow personal to Odysseus? When I turn back to ask the old art critic, he is gone.

The ride home is uneventful: the TSA lines, the usual change of planes in Houston. My little Lexus waits where I parked it at the Corpus Christi airport, and the drive over the causeway is, as always, an exercise in decompression. My little first floor condo is undisturbed and I toss my stuff onto the bed, change into my shorts, and throw a woven Mexican "drug rug" hoodie over my shirt. I slip into my "aloha slap" sandals and step out toward the beach for a walk, locking the door behind me. It's chilly, but not frigid like it was in New York.

I like winter at home: no surfers; no Spring Breakers; few humans – mostly old snowbirds from Illinois or Minnesota who claim to be fishing, but who are, in reality, worrying over their various ailments and wishing they had the money to be in Palm Beach or Fort Lauderdale. And hardly anyone walks the beach at dusk this time of year. Most of the tourists have gone inside to warm up by now.

I leave my slaps at the edge of the pavement, my bare feet hitting the cold sand. Waves roll in like muffled thunder. The falling sun streaks orange trails to the west, and a yellow moon rises over the ocean as I trudge on. I like to walk in the wet no-man's land between the ebbing and waxing waves. Here the starfish and sand dollars live and die and the tiny subterranean bivalve crustaceans filter their food from water they suck down the little chimneys they blow in the sand.

The beach feels almost deserted; just a few oldsters with ice chests or chairs ready to be packed up. I wave as I pass.

The next stranger is farther distant. The sun is almost gone and reveals only the outline of a lawn chair occupied by a figure with one knee crossed over the other: male or female? The top leg kicks in the air, a burnished silhouette of arched foot, pointed toe, slender ankle, and long calf. The form and the motion betray the truth even at this distance. I'll probably keep my head down. No point in making conversation. But at fifty paces the woman waves a greeting, and for reasons that are still unclear to me I veer up the sloping sand toward her. Maybe it just made sense to approach any sign of welcome.

I open with, "Do you like watching the sunset?"

"Yes it's beautiful."

"But you're facing the water. The sun's behind you."

"Doesn't matter; it's still beautiful," she says. "How about a beer?"

I haven't had an invitation like this in a while and I'm leery, but "sure," I say, even though I'm not crazy about beer. And when she hands me the bottle I tell her the half-truth that I am a writer. "I collect stories," I claim. "Tell me yours."

She introduces herself and shakes my hand, then invites me to sit in front of the shallow pit she has dug where a few small logs burn. The sand is cold, but soon the fire envelops us in warm pungent smoke.

"Where did you get the wood?" I ask.

"I bought it down the road. I try to think ahead."

She is plain and fortyish but not unattractive, visiting from Wisconsin, half German and half Japanese by ancestry she say, with short dark hair and almond shaped eyes. Two hours later, I feel I know her. Both her parents died young and she cries about that. She says she is happily married with three sons. By then we are lying face-up in the sand on opposite sides of the fire, gazing at stars in the indigo dark, and she has come to know me, too.

"Can't you relax?" she asks after I have finished both the beer and my complaints about life.

Am I shaking from the chill or my anxiety, or both? She downs her third glass of wine and moves closer. "Why are you so jittery? It's a beautiful night, and I'm not coming on to you," she promises, even as she reaches out and touches my shoulder ambiguously.

"I'm sorry; I'm afraid of everyone," I admit. "I don't trust anyone anymore."

"You aren't afraid of me, are you? We'll never see each other again."

"Yes," I say, "I am."

The full moon, now silver, hangs directly above us, encircled by a halo of cloud that expands outward in a spiral. My heartbeat and breathing begin to slow.

"I've never seen anything like that before," I whisper. "It's incredible…dome-like…makes me feel like I'm in a church."

"Hey," she responds, "pick a star, any star. Pick a star and make a wish."

I do, and we talk about it, and about our respective wishes and dreams, as the fire slowly burns out.

At some point the smoke begins to dissipate and I realize we have been here for hours, alone in the dark. Fear, an old friend, rises again within me. What if she has some scheme to entrap me or accuse me of something? How can I explain what we are doing here, even though it's totally innocent? What would I say if cross-examined by her husband? What would I advise a client in this situation?

I stand. "It's time for me to go."

She rises in response and I reach out to shake her hand again, this time in parting.

"Let's do one of these instead," she suggests, laying her

arms around my neck and leaning her torso into me. I glimpse an inquiry or invitation in her eyes, one I ignore. Instead I hug her closer to hide my face behind her shoulder, but she pulls back and kisses my temple chastely. "I hope you find what you are looking for," she says.

"Goodbye," I reply, already walking away toward my empty room. As the building's outline grows in the moonlight and I near the sidewalk, I can just hear music coming from the bar down the beach, Steely Dan:

> Well, the danger on the rocks is surely past.
> Still I remain tied to the mast.
> Could it be that I have found my home at last?
> Home at last?

Roberta Shellum Dohse

Roberta Shellum Dohse hails primarily from California. She is a graduate of the University of California Berkeley. After a stint on a farm in northern Minnesota and time in Oregon, she moved to Texas in 1980. She attended law school at the University of Houston and has practiced law in Corpus Christi, Texas since 1997. She was formerly a flight instructor and a college professor. She has always loved to write, and conveys her love of the land in her poetry.

Whispers

Something whispers in the wind
        and stirs in the dry leaves.
Cirrus clouds high above shift and bend.
        Uncomfortable.
Change. Is a storm coming?

I draw in, to watch closely as the dew gathers,
        as it swells on the lip of the small leaf.
The droplet glitters in the early morning sun,
        reflecting the sharp blue sky
        and the shapes around it.
Then it wavers, buffeted by the wind that
        scatters its images like a brilliant kaleidoscope.
It is overfull, and will soon fall.

I turn away first. I want only the memory,
        not the spilling,
             not the birth of what is to come.

Drought Along the Nueces

The land lifts, undulating, gently rolling higher,
Reaching for storm clouds in the distance.
The long rows of sorghum are plowed under,
    only a few remaining leaves to mark their passing,
Just as bundles of shriveled sticks
    that should have borne rich cotton
    lie hidden beneath thick clods of soil.
Now the land rests, awaiting new beginnings.
The land is life. But it thirsts. So dry.

A new freshness rises in the air,
    traveling with the breeze that lifts strands of my hair.
Glints of sunlight flash through gaps in the clouds,
    narrow shafts piercing the darkening afternoon,
    lending an other-worldly sense of suspended time.
Birds skitter across my vision,
    some bearing a light melody,
    others brashly cawing in mad swoops.
Wasn't I here yesterday?
    Yesterday when the dust hung thickly in the still air,
    when the light was flat and dull.
No anticipation then, no collective holding of breath.
Not like now.

Small animals peer out of burrows, sniffing cautiously.
Hawks soar, dive, then circle to soar again,
    reveling in the shifting currents of air.
The scent of rain grows as it moves ever closer.
Come to this place. Do not pass us by.
    We will welcome you.

Bittersweet

The old tree where you first pulled down a branch
   to pluck me a sweet blossom,
    where you first gazed so deeply into my eyes,
    it is leaning so wearily into the wind.

The old gas pump is still standing at the edge of town,
   though the station is now long abandoned.
It was there you first put your hands on my shoulders
   and drew me close, just to smell my hair.
And just up the hill is the old barn
   where we had our first dance,
    swaying so slowly to the rhythm of the band.
I still remember the deep musky smell of you.

There is music! And despite my best intentions,
   I am drawn in to gaze at the big dance floor,
   at the band at the far end, up on the stage,
    just getting started.
People filter in to sit at the rough wooden tables,
   laughing, talking,
    and I lose myself in the lively tunes.
I can almost taste the beer.
A smile steals across my lips.

Then a loud commotion erupts at the door,
   and you burst in,
    your bigger-than-life laugh filling this space.
You move through,
   greeting old friends, eyes sparkling,
   legs twitching with the pulsing rhythm.
The very air has come alive.

But you are not with me,
   and the tears spill unbidden from my eyes.
I stifle my sobs, fade back into the shadows,

then out into the twilight.
Still, I cannot keep from looking back as I drift
   slowly down the hill, and,
      like Lot's wife, I am rooted to the spot.

The last rays of the setting sun
   arc through the gaps in the walls,
      through the places where the roof has crumbled,
      where moss and leaves have tumbled in.
And, with a great a flutter of wings,
   a covey of dove bursts out into the cooling air.

Shadow and color mingle, and glitter in my tears.
When am I and where are you, my love?

The Upper Pasture

Shadows shift down below.
The creek has gone silent,
    and two sharp eyes glint back at me.
It is you, old friend?

I turn and walk away to the upper pasture,
    to catch the last of the evening sun
        as it glints through the haze of a blood red horizon.
I stay to watch the small white clouds thin
    and disappear into distant stars.

The scent is strong here.
Roe deer and fallow earth.
The sweat beads on my lip.

I lift my face to the gentle wind
    rising up from the lowlands,
        from the busy roads now mute in the distance.
It has tugged at the struggling crops and
    whispered to the grasses holding tight to the earth.
Now it soars out over the open country,
    lifting wings of the hawk,
    shooing flies away from the cattle
    making their way to the barn.
I taste the cedar, and hear the call of the cicadas.

Will you drift in on this wind to kiss me in greeting?
Or come up suddenly behind me,
    to catch me by surprise?
I will wait for you.

Chuck Etheridge

A self-proclaimed desert rat, Chuck Etheridge was raised in El Paso, Texas. After a stint in the US Navy keeping the coast of Southern California safe from the threat of enemy invasion, he attended the University of Texas at El Paso and Texas Christian University. In addition to his time in the service, he has worked as an actor, a convenience store clerk, a Rent-a-Poet, and a catalog copy writer before finding respectable employment as an English teacher, first at McMurry University and, later, at Texas A&M University-Corpus Christi. His poetry, fiction, and creative non-fiction have been published in a variety of reviews and anthologized in a number of books, and he has written two plays that have been produced. He is the author of two novels, Border Canto and The Desert After Rain. "Driving Lessons" is an excerpt of his third novel, My Father's Songs.

My Choice of Hells . . .

The Gods of the North warn
Hell is a hot place.
Do bad, and you will burn,
Smelling brimstone in a fiery pit
Forever.

South Texas sun blazes like an angry god,
Sweat runs rivers down my back,
My pale skin burns, red, so I must hide from the Sun,
Shield myself from the wrath of Thor
With sun hats, and sunblock,
While he burns my plants,
Evaporates lakes and rivers,
And slays even the toad
Crossing the parking lot,
Who dies, then swells up,
A grotesque balloon blistering on asphalt

This is summer.

Gods of the South snicker at the North,
Bask in the heat of Thor's wrath,
And warn,
Do bad and you will freeze,
In a dark cold place,
Forgotten.

Old Sol, the Sun, has grown weak
Forgetting Chicago in January.
I must work outside,
Stand in waist high snow,
Try to use a metal wrench
When it's twenty below zero.
The wind shoots down from the North,
Knifing my heart through the long underwear,
And heavy jacket. My hands, numb, can't work
With gloves on,
But can't work when they are frozen.
This is winter,
Quetzalcoatl's anger is everywhere,
Inescapable.

My southern bones fear Aztecs
More than Vikings,
Can always take clothes off,
But can't put on enough to keep warm.

If I have to choose hell, I'd rather be Aztec than Viking,
Would rather burn than freeze

Driving Lessons

Stevie popped her head into The Newsroom, what we grandiosely called the classroom where we produced the school paper. She had a big smile on her face. "Guess what!"

"What?" I asked, looking up from the typewriter, where I had just finished typing a story on the school's funky heating system.

She came over and plopped down on the table I was working at, her hair brushing me as she flew by. She was excited.

"We got out of Girl's Chorus early, so I called Mom while I was waiting for you. Mr. Herrera had left a message that it came in."

"Really?" I said, suddenly as excited as she was. "It's here?"

"Yeah!" she said, nodding her head fast and smiling.

Alex popped out of the darkroom, a stack of photos in his hand.

Stevie tugged my hand. "Come on," she said. "We have to hurry and catch the bus if we're gonna get there by five."

"Where do you need to go?" Alex asked.

I saw trouble and wasn't going to answer.

"Herrera's," said Stevie. "This really great Beatles retrospective came out and it has some songs you can't get anywhere else and all the lyrics and some new pictures -."

Miss Reynolds, our teacher, had stepped up then, nodding in that rare, unteacherly way that let you know that you were being listened to. "That sounds really fascinating. You ought to write a review, Pete."

"Really!?" I felt excited for a microsecond, then shook my head. "I don't know. I mean, I don't know how many people here at Central High like the kind of music we do."

Stevie was shaking her head in disagreement. "But maybe if you wrote a review, they might be interested."

"She's right," Miss Reynolds said. "You might change some minds."

It sounded good, but I was nervous about offering the music I loved up to the ridicule of the school. "Maybe," I said.

"Go ahead and catch the bus to the record store," she said.

"Your work here is done."

"I can give you a ride," Alex said.

"NO!" I said. "Uh, Alex, that's nice, but I know you have work to do."

Miss Reynolds said, "Go ahead, Alex. I can finish up." She thought she was being nice, I guessed, but I kept sending her telepathic signals to change her mind.

She didn't receive them.

Alex got his books. "Let's go."

As we walked out, I said, "Dude, this is really nice of you, but I don't want to be any trouble. We can catch the bus."

"If we do that, we'll barely make it," Stevie said.

There was no graceful way out of it. Maybe Stevie was so excited about the record that she'd forgotten everything I'd told her about Alex.

When we got to the car, Alex said, "Pete, be a gentleman. Let the lady ride in front."

I made a show of opening the door for her, and stepped very close so he wouldn't hear. "Stevie," I whispered.

"That tickles" she giggled, and reached for her ear with her hands.

"Don't worry, Pete," Alex said. "I know you guys want time together. I'll just drive around the block until you get done. I can wait."

"Gee, thanks," I said to him. Then I whispered to Stevie, "Do you love me?"

She looked at me oddly. "You know I do. You don't have to ask that."

"Then please wear your seatbelt."

She giggled out loud. "You're so funny," she said, and gave me a peck on the cheek.

"I'm serious. Promise me."

"Okay, okay, I promise," she said. But she gave me a funny look.

We got in the car. I buckled up, then Stevie did. Not Alex.

He started yakking about a story he was doing on how textbooks were chosen, and forgot to brake at the stop sign on Campbell, a busy one-way that heads down the hill south toward downtown El Paso. It was nearly five, early rush hour, and all three lanes of Campbell were full. He plowed straight across the traffic without braking.

Horns honked. Brakes squealed. Stevie squeaked, as she did when she was too shocked to make more noise.

"Oops," Alex said good-naturedly.

"Be careful, please," I pleaded.

"You are such a worry wart, Pete."

When he stopped on Stanton, he let too much of the car's front end stick out into the busy four-lane cross street. He said, "Uh, oh," and I turned and saw a big pickup bearing down. He threw the car in reverse and punched it.

HHHHHHHOOOOOOONNNNNKKKK. He jammed on the brakes so hard, all of our heads snapped forward. When I turned around, I saw that we'd nearly backed into a car that had pulled up behind us. We'd missed, but not by much.

"Guess I'm having a bad day," Alex muttered.

I kept my silence. So did she.

Then he started driving too cautiously, and wouldn't turn when he had time. We began to hear a lot of honking, and more and more cars pulled up behind him, blocked because he would not go.

"All right, already!" he yelled. He pulled across Stanton, very slowly, and crept down the hill doing about fifteen. I looked at the speed limit sign. It read thirty-five.

She turned to look at me then. Behind her glasses, her eyes were huge.

Her lips were moving silently. I realized she was praying.

We made it downtown without any more excitement, and had to cut over to Mesa when Stanton became one way heading back up the hill. He even managed to avoid the busses at the Plaza, and got into the mandatory right turn lane that would take us onto the street where Herrera's was.

I began to breathe more easily. Not to relax, but to breathe.

We turned and Alex began looking at shop fronts. "Let's, see, you said it was . . ."

"ALEX! LOOK OUT!" Stevie shrieked.

He jammed on the brakes and we all snapped forward again. He didn't come too close to the two men who were crossing the street -- maybe only about three feet. But it was a good thing Stevie had told him to stop.

He let the car hiccup forward until we were by the curb.

"Alex," Stevie said calmly. "Thanks a bunch for the ride." Then she looked back at me and said, "Pete, I just remembered my Mom said she needed me to go into Popular to get her more bath powder. That's too long for Alex to wait. We'll just take the bus home."

"I don't want you to have to do that," he said. "I don't mind."

She shook her head. "We don't want to take advantage," she said. "Thanks." She got out of the car.

"Thanks," I said, and scooted out, too.

We stood on the curb and waved as he drove off.

Then she clamped both hands on my arms so hard it hurt. "Omigosh, Pete! I was sooooo scared." Her eyes were all big again.

"I tried to warn you."

She nodded her head real fast again, and said, "I thought you were just teasing me about Alex. I didn't think anybody could drive that bad."

"Now do you believe me?"

She nodded again, this time more slowly, like she was making a point. Then she said, "Thanks for the tip about the seat belt."

I slipped my hand in hers. "You're welcome. But we'd better hurry if we're gonna go to Herrera's and have time to get the bath powder."

"What bath powder?" she said, grinning.

I laughed then. "Thanks."

"Pete?"

"Yeah?"

"I don't think we ought to let our kids drive right when they turn sixteen."

"Good plan," I said.

Devorah Fox

"What if?" Those two words all too easily send Devorah Fox spinning into flights of fancy. Her best-selling The Bewildering Adventures of King Bewilliam epic historical fantasy series includes The Redoubt, voted one of 50 Self-Published Books Worth Reading 2016, and The Lost King, awarded the All Authors Certificate of Excellence. She also wrote the historical thriller Detour, co-authored the contemporary thriller, Naked Came the Sharks, with Jed Donellie, contributed to Masters of Time: a SciFi/Fantasy Time Travel Anthology, and Magic Unveiled: An Anthology, and has several Mystery Mini Short Reads to her name.

An excerpt from **The Lost King**
Book One in The Bewildering Adventures of King Bewilliam

"Moo."

Moo? King Bewilliam frowned. What was a cow doing in the throne room?

"Moo."

King Bewilliam no sooner had set his gaze on the Bell Castle's richly-veined marble floors, the opulent woven tapestries, the straight lines of courtiers resplendent in their gold-braided uniforms than it all vanished.

His heart jolted and he felt a pervasive icy chill.

"Moo."

I'm asleep, the King thought. I'm dreaming. I need to wake up. He opened one eye. He had been dreaming but what vanished was not the cow but the throne room. Instead, the sight that greeted him was another eye: big, brown, and deep.

King Bewilliam opened his other eye and found himself face-to-face with a large Guernsey regarding him with mild curiosity.

"Moo, moo," said the cow although to the king it sounded distinctly like "Who, you?" which, it seemed to him, was an excellent question given the circumstances. Was he not King Bewilliam, ruler of the Chalklands, master of Bell Castle? So what was he doing here staring down a cow? He shook his head to clear the fog of slumber. One by one, the details of his surroundings impressed themselves on him: the cool, moist dawn air; the dewy grass on which he lay; the dark canopy of the oak tree arching over him. And the cow.

King Bewilliam eased into a sitting position and looked about. In the thin light of daybreak he saw many cows grazing in the pasture that surrounded him. What was he doing sleeping in a cow pasture? his waking mind struggled to know.

Oh yes, it was where he had come to rest after walking all day. He hadn't talked to a single person, having kept his distance, avoiding questions about who he was and what he was doing here. He knew who he was: first-born son of a noble line, raised to rule, trained to lead and now, a grown man, husband to Queen Daya, and father of princes. What he was doing here in this unfamiliar place, his crown nowhere to be found, his fine tunic and leggings tarnished and soiled, his boots scuffed, was a mystery to him.

Well, an inquisitive cow wasn't all that unfortunate an encounter. At least there would be breakfast. He rummaged his mug from the pouch at his belt, then hesitated. He scanned the area for onlookers who might accuse him of poaching. There were none.

"Here, Boss." He stroked the cow's sturdy flank to gentle her, then milked her. As he worked, he observed how strange many might find it that a king would, much less could, milk a cow. Certainly, Bell Castle's milkmaid who had shown him how had thought so. Yet even as a young prince, the workings of things fascinated him. He would pester every maid, knave, squire, knight, and lady to show him the why and how of what they did.

His meager breakfast done, he turned the ermine-lined cloak that had been his bed inside out and knotted the ends together, making it into a shoulder sack. It would have been easier to wear the weighty cloak across both shoulders than to lug it on one but he knew he mustn't be seen wearing it. No one would believe that a vagabond like him rightfully owned such a fine garment. It would be seized and he might be imprisoned as a thief. Nevertheless, he was reluctant to part with it. The cloak had served well as bedding when he found himself sleeping out in the open.

He finger-combed the grass from his red curls and observed that his hair had gotten unseemly long. So had his beard, he discovered as he ran his hand over his face. When he reached a town, he would need to visit a barber. First, however, he would need to raise some money to pay a barber, not to mention buy a decent meal. His stomach growled in agreement. Apparently the birds had beaten him to the berries. He quickly banished from his mind the image of the generously-laid groaning boards to which he was accustomed before it could further exacerbate his hunger.

He sighed, hefted his improvised sack, and set off.

The morning sun had strengthened by the time King Bewilliam spied the first sign of civilization. In the distance, a farmer's oxcart made slow progress across the horizon. King Bewilliam strained to see clearly. It was headed toward town, he surmised, as the wagon was laden. He aimed his feet in the same direction and hurried his pace in hopes of overtaking the cart and begging a ride. He was already tired of walking and the day had barely begun.

"Eh! Friend! Where are you bound?" he called when the driver was in earshot.

The wooden cart slowed but did not stop. The driver turned his head, showing a long face shadowed by a broad-brimmed hat.

"To market, of course, Stranger," the driver replied.

"Is it far?" asked Bewilliam.

"Far enough." The driver sounded weary. "And my long day truly begins only when I get there. I don't have time to waste chatting with strangers."

"Perhaps some entertainment would make your journey pass more enjoyably." King Bewilliam withdrew a harmonica from his pouch and whistled a phrase, light and sweet as the chirping of the red-breasted robins roosting in the trees that lined the wagon way.

The cart slowed yet more.

"A pretty tune, but how do I know this isn't some ruse to rob me?" the driver asked.

King Bewilliam flung his arms away from his body. "I have only this knife for a weapon which I would entrust to you for the length of the journey." He was close enough now to see the driver's eyes narrow in concentration.

"And that sack of yours?"

Were it not for his sack's ermine secret, Bewilliam would have offered to allow the driver to search for weapons. "I'll give you custody of that too," he said and came alongside the wagon.

The wagon stopped. "Hand them over, then," the driver said, "and climb aboard. And play another tune. You do pull some fine notes from that thing."

King Bewilliam did as bidden. He settled himself in the rope sling strung from the cart's side and appraised the cart's load. "Radishes," he said, inhaling the spicy, earthy aroma.

"Aye."

"I like radishes," King Bewilliam said. "These are rather small...no offense."

"None taken. Would that I could grow them bigger."

"Hmm. Have you tried feeding the earth with the refuse of your meal from the night before?"

The farmer frowned. "Would that help?"

King Bewilliam explained that apparently when certain items such as onion peels and melon rinds rotted, they returned beneficial humours to the soil, so the decomposed refuse could be used as fertilizer. "But don't use meat scraps or bones. That just attracts vermin."

The farmer pursed his lips and nodded. "How know you this? Do you farm?"

King Bewilliam shook his head and smiled. "I like radishes."

"Have you one, then," replied the farmer. "Then play me a tune, Friend." He put out his hand. "I am John."

No "Your Majesty," no bow. King Bewilliam had not encountered many people lo these unnumbered days of wandering but when he had, not a single one offered anything more than the most common of courtesies. It was taking some getting used to. No one took him for anything more than what he seemed to be: a vagrant. The only part of his appearance that merited any attention was his footwear. Though shabby, his boots were somewhat grander than the flimsy slipper-type shoes most plebeians wore, suggesting that he had seen better days. That was certainly true.

His own hand halfway toward accepting the greeting, King

Bewilliam stammered, "I'm... I'm..." He took a cue from the birds that had inspired his tune. "Robin."

They shook hands. With the slap of the chains, John put the cart in motion. "From whence you come, Robin? A far piece, from the looks of you."

Robin nodded. "A far piece." In miles, an untold number. Much farther than that in terms of what he had left behind and where he now found himself. He dusted the soil from the radish and ate it in one bite. "You might have left the radishes in the ground longer."

"Would that I could have, but I have a need for cash. I have a loan that's come due."

They rode for three songs and one lengthy tale that Robin told of a night in a tavern. It so amused the farmer that he cried with laughter. Then Robin took the reins while Farmer John slept. Jouncing in the cart's rope-sling seat didn't do Robin's bottom any favors. He wished for the gentler ride of Bell Castle's royal carriages with their cushioned seats and a springy suspension that he had invented. His feet were grateful for the rest, however, and riding spared his already shabby boots.

The morning was warm, warmer than he remembered spring mornings being. Maybe it was no longer spring, but summer or fall. Had he been walking that long? It felt like a lifetime. However the tender green of the leaves on the trees and shrubs told him that they were still in the earlier part of the year.

"Eh, Farmer John, I believe we're nearing town."

John raised his head.

"Must be Market Day from the looks of all this traffic," said Robin. The number of farmers and merchants using the wagon way had gradually increased until it had become quite crowded.

"Nay, this is only Tuesday," said Farmer John. "It's often like this."

"Indeed?" Robin handed over the reins.

"This is a popular trade center."

Clearly it was. The carts alongside them were heaped with produce and goods.

"I hope to sell the entire load," John said.

His face was tight and Robin suspected the debt that the farmer owed preyed on his mind. "The loan of which you spoke?"

The farmer nodded. "Yes. I had a drainage problem at the farm. My fields flooded with every rain and my crops were ruined."

"Your lord was not inclined to help?" I would have been, Robin thought. After all, his fortunes rose and fell with those of his tenants.

"I own my land," John said. "It's not much but it is mine, and I am proud to be able to bequeath it to my sons when the time comes. Farming here is a challenge. Our weather is downright devilish. Some days are brutal hot, others bitter cold. Sometimes we have terrible storms with great winds. We have droughts followed by downpours that could drown an ox. This last deluge about swept me away." He shook his head. "I was told, 'Send word to Lord Bernard.' And yes, I had heard that this lord had provided assistance to others, for an obligation. One day I was approached by one of his knights who said that I needed to dig a ditch. Well of course I did, but I didn't have the wherewithal to do it."

Robin nodded. Farmers, he knew, were busy from sunup to sundown and beyond just getting the farming done, much less making capital improvements.

"Before long," said John, "the knight returned with a small loan for me. It was just enough for me to hire a ditch digger."

"And now?"

"My crops have been doing much better. It looked like I was going to be in a position to pay back the loan as agreed but the knight visited me and told me that Lord Bernard demands payment now."

That didn't sound at all right to Robin. What was the worth of an agreement if both parties did not honor the terms? "Perhaps you are dealing with a rogue knight who seeks to fill his own pouch."

Farmer John shook his head. "I don't think so. He seemed to regret having to pressure me, and I think was fearful of what would happen if he didn't return to Lord Bernard with money." John frowned. "You have not heard of Lord Bernard?"

"No, I can't say that I have."

The farmer shrugged. "No matter. I hope to get out from under this obligation and then truly, I have learned my lesson. I will make the best of what I have and not aspire beyond my means."

Alongside the road, a trellis covered with rambler roses

marked the settlement ahead. To Robin, the absence of a defensive ditch, wall, or gate spoke of a loosely-organized settlement not even worthy of the term "village."

"That's Rose Bank, the trade center, up ahead," said Farmer John. He handed Robin his sack and knife. "Where go you from here, Friend?" he asked as Robin dismounted the wagon.

"Don't know." It would be helpful if he knew where he was.

All he could remember was walking. Perhaps he had set out for a hike. There was nothing unusual about his leaving the castle. He often toured the countryside, partly to escape the pressure of court and partly to see firsthand how fared his subjects. However, rarely did he go without his retinue and most assuredly did not go on foot.

This last time, apparently, he had set out alone, walked beyond the castle gates, and kept walking. He remembered walking and walking and walking until he could walk no more, sat to rest, and fell asleep. He awoke and realized that he was in a strange land, definitely out of his realm. Could he have been enchanted while he slept? An enchantment would explain his lot. If not a spell, what other reason could there be for his mysterious transformation from honored and respected ruler to homeless vagabond?

He remembered trying to make his way back to his kingdom. Yet the harder he tried, the further he got into unknown territory. He sorely missed the ease and luxury of royal life. He felt adrift in the absence of challenges presented to him daily, and the satisfaction of reaching solutions where benefits outweighed the cost. He tried not to think about his wife and two sons as that brought a longing that was too painful to bear.

If he even could make it back to his realm, what would he find? Did his family and subjects await his return? Would the kingdom have fallen to ruin? Had he been deposed? Did someone else now rule in his place? If that were true, would he even be able to reclaim his throne? Certainly it would take more than simply reappearing, ragged and worn from life on the road. Hell, he might need an army to recapture his throne. At the very least, he would need a king's ransom to redeem it.

A king's ransom. What a joke! At the moment he didn't have a coin to buy a haircut or a crust of bread to eat or a bed in which to sleep. He sighed. Here in this settlement there would be no sleeping in the open, for he would be arrested as a vagrant. Perhaps, though, he could find some employment and raise a few coins.

Paul Gonzales

Paul Gonzales is an award winning journalist for The News of San Patricio weekly newspaper as well as an award winning filmmaker. He's currently working on his second novel and seeking representation for his first novel and various short stories and novellas. He currently resides in Corpus Christi with his wife and two children.

Transplants

I heard the beeps first. Machines placed around me somewhere in the dark buzzed, whirled and wheezed. Then I felt the needles sticking out from my skin pumping fluids through my veins, all of them swollen. My skin was sore. My chest was separated under bandages and stitches and blood and exposed marrow and healing arteries and I wondered what color my blood was down in there. I imagined the highways of vessels crisscrossing under my chest plate turning the blue blood red as it was exposed underneath the still fresh wound splitting my chest in two even pieces, soaking up the stale hospital air. With eyes closed and hands still, I tried to feel around the room. Tried to sense someone or something. My ears listened. My nose sniffed. Eyelids twitched. Only machines and tubes that dripped and flowed and stabbed and the one that breathed for me. I had nothing else to do but sleep. But I didn't do that.

****

I lay there staring out a window that faced another wing of the hospital. Dirty peach. That was the color I came up with. That was the color of the brick caked onto the ancient hospital. Nurse. Jell-O. New sheets. Dirty peach. For days that was it. I could hear the nurses whisper about my lack of visitors and how a bad heart at such a young age was such a shame. And I lay there thinking and looking out the window and listening to my new heart hammer on the inner walls of my chest.

When I got home I could see my neighbors peach tree from out of my bedroom window. Overgrown and filled with rotting peaches. He once asked me if I liked the fruit and I had told him no. So I watched the tree from my bed, my body still too weak to move about much, so alone in my house watching autumn transform the landscape, it was the same view. Rotting peach. That was the color I came up with.

****

There was a cake on the break room table already cut and missing pieces when I walked in. The boss and the other two employees leaned against the counter laughing and shouting, showering themselves with chocolate. They noticed me and offered some of my welcome back surprise cake. "Surprise!" I thought. "There's still some left!"

My desk was almost bare except for my computer monitor and my pencil holder, which was the opposite of how I left it. Full. I was able to return to work as long as I took over Feather's secretary position. She had gone into labor three days ago and still hadn't blessed us with Rocko Firth Shapiro Warren. For some reason that's what I figured its name would be, but I hadn't paid attention enough to even know what the sex of the baby was. I just needed to get out of the house. My chest was still tight and sore so I couldn't do any hard physical activities. Not that my former activities at the office could be anywhere near the realm of being called an activity much less be referred to as physical. So I sat and answered phones, took messages and from time to time I found myself staring out of the window facing the street. One minute I would be helping clients fill out forms, then the next I was watching the passersby scuttle across a cold, wet street through a foggy, ice covered window.

I blamed my lack of attention on the drugs I had long since stopped taking. And at night I felt like an old tin chamber in the shape of a man with warm coals glowing deep inside. It was a calming, lonely feeling. Then I began seeing places I hadn't ever seen before play against the insides of my eyelids as I counted breaths in an effort to sleep. And they played on, even when I did manage to sleep. Street signs. Stores. People. All too real, familiar, yet alien. And when sleep eluded me and my eyes were open, images danced on the darkened ceiling and walls of my bedroom.

The doctor's office was cold. The hard white sheet of what must be butcher paper was pulled across the examination table and wrinkled underneath me, making a loud rustling sound that filled the empty room. A nurse walked in.

"Everything seems fine," she said through pale, dry lips. "Your body's taking to the transplant quite well. Just don't do any strenuous activities and don't exert yourself too much."

I nodded and began to button up my shirt. "Umm, excuse me nurse," I said in a voice much lower than I had planned. She looked up from her clipboard. "Sometimes it feels like...well, my heart beats harder than I think it should."

She lowered the clipboard to her hip. "After what kind of activities?"

I straightened up concerned. "When I'm just, like, driving or sitting at my desk at work. Even when I'm sleeping. It doesn't hurt or anything, it's just hard. Harder than usual. And sometimes loud. Is that normal?"

The nurse smiled, causing the corners of her eyes to make crow's feet. "Oh yes, that's normal. You're just not used to your new heart yet. Some hearts have more muscle than others. Like people. Some more, some less. You must have gotten a strong one. But don't worry sugar, you'll get used to it. Oh, and don't forget to sign out at the front. Thank you and have a good day."

I got up to my feet and counted the thumps. Normal. It's normal she said. But it felt hot and hollow down inside. Past the other parts that squeezed and pushed and filtered and breathed. The warm coals down inside the chamber pulsed like they were reaching and grasping out. I walked out with my fingers crawling across my chest trying to figure it. My thoughts rummaged through my innards like a lost explorer in a jungle. There was a voice. Louder and louder the closer I came to the exit.

I was called back in. I forgot to sign out.

The following day I found myself looking over city maps as they flashed on my computer screen from behind my secretary desk, studying the street names and memorizing the turns and landmarks. Some sounding strangely familiar, others completely new. Satellite images from space slid out of the printer and I poured over them as if I knew what it was I was looking for. I glanced up from the screen to the clock then back to the screen then back again as my fingers clacked away on the keys.

My boss stepped in and said he had a doctor's appointment and that I would be left in charge for the rest of the day. I watched from my secretary desk's window and waited for him to pull away in his fancy car before sending the phone calls to the answering service and grabbing my bag.

****

I began finding myself in places I hadn't been before, but every step taken was increasingly familiar. I controlled only my eyes and mouth. My steps took themselves. Sometimes into alleys and back out again. Over sidewalks and across intersections. Sometimes surefooted, sometimes lost or confused. And after a day's walk around foreign neighborhoods, following work usually, we'd mark our place and start from there the next day, my feet and I. Today our mark would be a street lamp.

I'd yank and curse like a mad man in the night until reluctantly my feet would give up control and we'd walk back to the car. Under highway lights and moonlit skies we'd drive back home. It had been a few days, almost a week now, but it was habitual. The relinquished control of bodily movements to uncover some meaning behind the walking and running and turning and pacing and stopping. Lungs pumping under my still newly imported muscle. That was it. The strings that pulled these marionette's legs onward. It was the fist-sized core buried inside this cavity of bone and blood that drove my body through the streets. Wanting. Searching. Lost out there like myself.

My foot pressed down on the accelerator firmly. The street lamp marker flew by. My hands turned the steering wheel to the left and to the right. I managed to slow down the car a bit to at least maintain some sense of control over the situation before we killed ourselves, my heart and I. The maps and streets and blue colored roads and pixilated treetops passed before my eyes as my hands flipped blinkers on and turned corners and my feet pumped the gas and brake simultaneously, skipping and lunging in front of houses and apartment buildings and laundromats and record shops.

I just stared out the windshield, shrugging my shoulders, as crowded sidewalks stared back in confusion. Then my car veered into a parking space and screeched to a halt next to a meter with a brown bag placed over it. My chest felt as if was about to burst. Shotgun blast thumps pounded the insides of my chest plate. I tried to get out but my hands had fully turned against me and refused to release the wheel. My feet remained planted to the floorboard of the car. I watched out of the window as people continued to pass. I studied and browsed and stared as my chest exploded beneath the long vertical scar that ran down my torso. Something was here. This was my destination, but where was the X that marked the spot? What is it that brought me here? Seconds ticked past as my eyes bounced back and forth through the crowds. Was it a boy? A girl? A pet? A house? A car? A store? What?! My eyes refused to blink and began to burn red. Fingers gripped the wheel and sweat trickled down my brow. My pupils dilated.

Across the street, a girl holding a shopping bag with a large, crooked red X printed over some sickly models wearing barely anything, slid into view. My chest froze. My new heart was silent. My hands reached for the door handle. My eyes, engulfed in flames, studied her every move. Her walk. Her flowing hair. Her hands. Clothes. Nothing was familiar about her but her.

My feet stumbled over themselves and over the asphalt. My chest bounded me forward in unyielding steady pounds after the girl marked with an X. Cars honked and drivers yelled as I stumbled towards her like a drunk chasing booze, a bullet chasing its target. I had never seen her before but I could feel a connection bursting from within. So hot and boiling and bubbling and shifting. Waves were washing over inside me causing my skin to burn hot. She was on her steps now fishing for her keys with the bag sliding down her forearm. My eyes were focused beams. I bumped and shoved my way through the people littering the sidewalk, excusing myself without looking away from her. Their curses grew silent. Violent gestures blurred and faded. My hand reached out. My heart made its ways through the bones and tissue and pressed firmly against my skin. My feet stopped. I stood behind her as she opened her building's door. My shoulders pumped forward viciously.

My hand reached out further and fingernails scraped old paint. The door had closed behind her.

My upper body stopped. My mouth open, yet silent. My

eyes welled-up from the steam bellowing inside, searching for release. My breath came back rigid, thick and quick. My hand twisted the doorknob frantically. It didn't turn.

But, from the other side of the door, a heavy thumping sound could be heard. Muffled but still audible. And my chest cavity lashed out a cry of hope. Blood rushed through my body at breakneck speeds causing color to leave my skin for a moment. I became a washed-out ghost pressed against a stranger's door. A stranger who shared the same heartbeat I could now hear clearly as the pounding grew louder. Closer. Closer. Closer. And my eyes watched a blurred figure grow larger through the decorated glass.

Cautiously she drew herself closer. The explosions grew louder. And slowly the sounds fell into time with one another as the door creaked open. First a face. Eyes. Nose. Lips. Her deep red hair framing gorgeous features. Her torso pumped her forth, out of the doorframe onto mine like amazing magnets and our chambers connected beneath our sweaters. Smashing chests and meeting scars. A beautiful collision. Fire was everywhere.

And our lips met. She clawed my waist with wanting fingers. My hands gently cradled her face. The threads of our sweaters intertwined and knitted themselves into one. Their belts unbuckled and leather whipped about. Their shoelaces twirled below them like snake lovers crazy with lust. And her lips called and mine answered. Our beats finely tuned instruments in this two-piece orchestra bathed in flames and burnt foliage. Strangers here underneath the falling leaves of autumn.

I could feel her lips curl at their ends as they pressed against mine. Her chest kicking hard and violent against my own. Exchanging beats and thumps and pounds and pushes and pulls and explosions and pumps and pulses.

Our hearts meet once again.

Scott Wayland Griffin

Scott Wayland Griffin has traveled internationally and lived in other parts of the U.S. He returned to his hometown and works as an industrial mechanic. Hobbies include medieval re-enactments, blacksmithing and creative writing.

Two Wolf Pups

Moshadoe & Mohirae quickly learned the finer arts of hunting with the pack under the watchful eye of Garoun. They were allowed to follow the hunters at a respectful distance at a much younger age than usual.

Sadly, not all the older wolves appreciated having two pups tagging along. One in particular, named Badu, took every opportunity to snap at the young pair. He wasn't very bright himself and he'd had a tough time learning the skills of a hunter. When he was young, he'd been picked on by Garoun for making mistakes that usually cost the pack a missed kill.

Badu's mistakes were pretty serious and as such, he deserved a little nip on the nose or a bite on his ear because that's the way wolves treat idiots who lost the pack a meal. Garoun wasn't being mean about it, he was just handling the situation in the traditional manner.

Some wolves hold a grudge however and Badu was one of them. In his dim memory, he remembered the bites and nips being much worse than they really were and he also imagined that his mistakes were not so very bad. So, when Garoun brought the pups along, Badu took much pleasure in biting them every chance he got.

If Mohirae breathed too loud, Badu would snap at her and loudly tell her to stop being too loud, "You'll scare away the rabbits!" Of course, Badu was much louder than her little puppy breathing would ever be. If Badu was scratching an itch and he saw Moshadoe scratching too, he'd stop scratching just so he could bite Moshadoe's ear & tell him gruffly, "Stop scratching! You'll scare away the deer!"

All this the two pups endured and more, but the worst thing that Badu would do came after every successful hunt.

When a pack brings down a deer or elk, the older hunters get first turn at eating. Once they have grabbed what they wanted then the others could come take bites, according to each wolf's status in the pack. The youngest and smallest always had to wait till the last to get a small bite and Moshadoe & Mohirae knew this. They almost always waited to take their rightful turns, but Badu would bite at them and drive them away, snarling that he still wasn't finished eating. He would eat slowly, sometimes not really eating at all, only gnawing noisily on a bone as he tormented the pups by announcing how tasty this deer or that elk was.

If Garoun noticed he would shake his head in disgust with Badu. He would sometimes still have some scraps left from his part of the kill and he'd let them finish it, but he couldn't stop Badu because that wasn't how things worked. If he tried to force Badu into letting the pups eat before all the other wolves were done, it would cause a terrible fight. The tradition of taking turns according to one's status in the pack was not a thing to interfere with and if Badu said he wasn't done then the pups had to wait. The trouble was that by the time Badu grew tired of his game, one of the other wolves would resume eating and the pups would still be sitting there, waiting with rumbling bellies. Several times the pups would get nothing at all to eat from the pack's kill.

One day the pack had brought down a deer that was too small to feed all the larger wolves so the pups knew they wouldn't even get a bone to gnaw on. Moshadoe turned to Mohirae and said, "Let's go see what kind of food we can hunt on our own. There might be some rabbits near the frozen lake."

As they made their way along the path, they noticed several other wolves were hunting up mice and rabbits in the area. "Let's go farther, we don't want anyone telling us we scared away the mice by making too much noise" said Mohirae.

The two traveled on until they reached the very edge of the frozen lake. At the same instant, a large old rabbit emerged from his hole right in front of them. They stared at each other for a second before the rabbit leaped, heading away on the icy surface of the lake with the two hungry wolf pups hot on his tail. They slipped all over the place but finally managed to trip up the rabbit and then the hunt was over. The pups began to sing the song of the pack to celebrate their kill, but the rough growls of Badu made them stop. Turning around, they saw him coming towards them over the ice. "Don't be singing over that rabbit, he's mine" growled the older wolf.

It looked like he'd be taking their dinner, until the ice broke from under Badu and sent him into the freezing water below. He paddled around in circles trying to pull himself back onto the ice. He called to them, "Help me out you little runts, my tail is frozen." Moshadoe told him, "We will gladly help you, just as soon as we're done with this tasty little rabbit."

As the two pups ran off with their rabbit, they could hear Badu snarling at them as he tried to pull himself from the water. "I'm going to have that rabbit, it's mine I say!"

The pups went back up the path a little way before they began eating near a thorny cactus. They'd almost finished when a very unhappy and frozen Badu caught up to them. Moshadoe dropped the rabbit remains and it landed on the cactus. He snarled in his little pup voice, "Leave us alone. That rabbit is so small that a big hunter like you could swallow it whole. Well I won't let you, it's ours!"

Mohirae looked at Moshadoe in shock, she couldn't believe he had just talked to an elder in that tone. He whispered to her, "Just watch, he'll eat it now for sure."

The pup's torment worked. Badu was so angry that he pounced on the rabbit and indeed, he tried to swallow it in just one bite. That was all it took, for in his greed he had grabbed the small cactus in his mouth also. As he felt the long thorns stabbing at the insides of his mouth, Badu went cross-eyed and his ears went up in surprise. He tried to push the evil thorny rabbit from his mouth with his tongue, but the needles pierced that as well. He managed to pry the cactus and rabbit from his mouth with his paws, but they too suffered injury. Now he had thorns in his paws, his mouth, and his tongue. He was in no mood to cause trouble for the pups as he slunk away with his tail tucked between his back legs in shame. In fact it was days before Badu was able to eat anything and he never again tried to stop the pups from eating with the pack. He no longer snapped at them or bit their ears, for he had learned his lesson and had lost his taste for rabbits, all in the same day.

Kailey Morgan Hamauei

Born in Corpus Christi and raised somewhere between her grandmother's Arabic kitchen, the public library, and the Padre Island National Seashore, Kailey Morgan Hamauei still calls the Coastal Bend her home. She put herself through school to study literature at Del Mar College and is currently pursuing her equal passion in animation. She has pursued other creative work, most recently as a comic book artist and actress in a film produced by the locally based Night Creature Productions. Her passion is storytelling in any medium. Her contribution to this anthology is her public debut in writing.

The Wedding

The pale amber liquid swirled around in Sam's highball glass, the dark color of the whiskey diluted by the melting ice cubes. A cacophony of conversations and laughter passed by him; the men in tuxedos and women in glittering evening wear drifted back and forth between the dancefloor and the bar. Glasses, gleaming golden and filled to the brim with champagne, clinked together in toasts he could not hear over the music. Occasionally someone would clap him on the back or stop to exchange some quick banter, but with the exception of moving to get another drink, he had stood all evening fixed to his position near the bar.

He drained the last of his drink in one swallow. The back of his throat seized up and burned a little in protest but he relished the feeling. Cate had not finished her drink yet. In fact, she had probably only taken maybe two sips from what he could see. She looked older now than she had, not so much in features, but in the distinguished and deliberate way she carried herself. From where he stood and because of the dim lighting he could not tell how the details of her face had changed through the years, but he knew there had to be changes. His own face had changed a little more than he liked to admit. He had to shave every day now to keep his face smooth. There was a large crease that appeared between his eyebrows now when he moved them and that lingered even when he didn't. He couldn't remember having that as a teenager. He also couldn't remember the little lines around his eyes or when they had appeared.

He wondered if the red of her hair simply looked muted because of the lighting, or if it had lost its fire and begun to tame with age. He wondered if the kid had red hair too.

It was time for another drink. He was certainly not the only one taking advantage of the open bar. God knows how much dough Jackie and Frank laid down for this shindig. As much as Sam tried to avoid weddings, he always seemed to be getting invited to them. He hadn't even realized his social circle was that big until everybody started getting hitched. He was always invited. He was a popular guy. People always tried to find a girl for him though, and he didn't like that. He could get a date on his own if he wanted. Trouble is he didn't want to. He had no desire to. He tried, he did, but it never felt right. Women expected too much. Everyone always just wanted to go steady. What was the trouble in dancing for a night, having a drink, or catching a flick? Taking a woman to a wedding was a kiss of death on any relationship that wasn't a serious one as far as he was concerned. Now it was his kid sister's turn to tie the knot and he had to go to this one. Christ, he was in this one. He didn't think he and Cliff had really hit it off when they met, which was probably only twice before the wedding, but he certainly didn't expect to be asked to be a groomsman. Jackie put him up to it he was sure. Or maybe Cliff was just the kind of guy that was sentimental like that.

Jackie'd never forgive me if I'd missed it. He thought of how happy she looked during the ceremony. She was wearing their mother's gown. It had to be taken in a quite a bit before it fit her but she looked swell in it. When Cliff saw her walking down that isle, his face was flushed redder than Christmas lights. Maybe he wasn't such a show-off after all.

But then Cate was here too. He hadn't anticipated that. Christ almighty, it had been clear over a decade since he'd seen her. He spotted her at the beginning of the reception with her big happy dunce of a husband Ted standing not too far off with a coupe glass of pale, bubbling champagne. Ted, that moron, Ted that big putz. She obviously saw Sam during the ceremony. He was in the ceremony for Christ's sake. Had she been watching him this whole time, careful to keep her distance? Careful to not finish her drink so that she wouldn't have to get another one and come nearer to him?

In truth, Sam could probably remember a time when he loved Ted. He was always a good guy to have around, a swell neighbor, as far as neighbors went. He taught Sam a lot of things his own father hadn't bothered to, from changing tires, to fixing this or that around the house. Ted knew how to do it all, which was pretty impressive for a travelling salesman. Ted and Cate moved across the street on old Riverberry Road when Sam was fifteen. They could still live there for all he knew, he hadn't been back to visit in years, he made sure of it. Work helped him with that. He also made sure not to ever ask about them, unless brought up. He knew about the kid. His mother had told him. He had already moved out when he got the news that Cate was having a baby -- a girl no less. It seemed unreal. Sam was scared at first; horrified really. Imagining Cate like...that -- all full and swollen, waddling around -- was something he had difficulty doing, and when he tried, he found no warmth in the thought. Pregnancy is nothing he knew anything about. Like most men, he now knew. When his own mother was pregnant with Jackie, he never paid much attention. The affairs of women were not a thing any boy should concern himself with. At least that's what his Pa would say. But Ma had said that Cate's baby was beautiful with green eyes had reminded her of Sam when he was a baby. There was no reason for Ma to mention the girl over the years, but every now and then Sam would hear a bit of information. She was a teenager by now. Or close to it. He shuddered involuntarily.

Ted and Catherine had been married for five years with no children, and suddenly a goddamn miracle? He didn't buy it. He didn't have the guts to ask her...but he didn't buy it. The only thing his dad had bothered to mention about women is that if you weren't careful, you could get them in real trouble. After seeing the alterations that needed to be made on Jackie's wedding dress, Sam realized that his father had really meant what he said about "real trouble".

The thing about Ted's job was that it kept him away from home a lot. Maybe everything had just been a recipe for disaster from the beginning.

The goddamn of it was that Sam became sweet on Cate. Not

on purpose or anything like that. At first he just hung around his neighborhood doing odd jobs for everyone. If a lawn needed to be mowed, a thing like that, Sam was there to make a quick buck. Summer breaks meant work, like a hot sun meant sweat. He liked having a bit of extra spending money, and he didn't mind menial tasks, so if old man Greenburg needed his hedges trimmed or the dogs taken out, Sam was there.

Ted and Catherine had a lot of little repairs to do to their house when they bought it. The neighborhood wasn't exactly a new one, and they certainly weren't the first folks to live there. Ted didn't like Cate doing manual labor, so Sam helped regularly. They gave the exterior of the home a fresh coat of crisp white paint as well redoing the rooms on the inside, one by one, tailoring this and that to suit their liking, or to Ted's liking anyway. Cate simply nodded him along when he pitched his ideas to her. The trouble really started when Ted got the idea in his head to build a nursery. He assured Sam that he was certain that he and Cate would be parents sometime real soon and that he wanted to be ready for it...but a year passed, and there was still no baby. There were only cradles to be built, furniture to be stripped and painted and reupholstered. Sam found himself at their house more than his own at times, and that was whether Ted was home or not.

Sam had a familiarity with Cate that was unlike that with Ted. Cate was observing and quiet unless spoken directly to. She could be a real joker and kid you around when she wanted to. She had a laugh that showed just the right amount of her straight, pearly teeth. For the most part though, Cate kept her ideas to herself. Her inner commentary was private. She was an artist with a pencil or brush and when she looked at people, she really looked at them; and that was something even Sam could see. When her pale blue eyes lingered on Sam, he imagined they seared. He would feel his breath catch in his throat if she looked too long, and that was when he started seeing Cate as more than just Ted's wife, but as a force entirely unknown and dangerous of its own accord.

Sam always found himself trying to win one of those big smiles from her, yet they appeared less frequently. That afternoon was a blur to him, something that could only be remembered in colors and smells. She had been painting. Some landscape, he thought, though he couldn't remember the details. The nursery had been long finished but Sam found himself coming over frequently even when there was no work to be done.

She washed green paint from her hands in the sink, and then sipped her Seagram's 7 from the chipped highball that was her favorite. Sam remembered the taste of it on her lips, the smell of the acrylics, the soft brush of her flaming hair on the whiteness of his chest; he remembered the blue of the eyes that could both burn and drown him.

To think now about the kid...his kid – made his head reel. Would Cate ever tell her about him? Would she tell Ted? He could not imagine himself being a dad. Unlike Ted, he had not longed for that kind of responsibility. And hell, Ted looked happy.

Sam's heart caught in his throat for a moment. If he had drunk a little less, his nerves would have overtaken him. Cate made her way toward the bar, her drinking glass finally empty. It was a slow approach as she worked the room. Several others greeted her as she walked with her navy blue glittering wrap catching the light. When she finally got close to him, he received her graciously enough. She kissed him, carefully pressing very close to his lips instead of the far cheek, like most women did. She asked him how he was and he asked her the same. The hundred things he wanted to tell her, to ask her, curdled in the forefront of his mind...he could not bring himself to say any of it. She knew that he knew. Not by anything she said of course, but in the way her eyes searched him. He could not hold her gaze for long, he didn't have the ability.

"It was great to see you, Sam," she said.

"I know," he replied. The words tumbled. Cate looked at him again, full in the eyes. The edges of her nostrils flared in the smallest of increments. "I know..." he repeated.

This time it was he who kissed her. On the cheek. Boldly, quickly. Joyfully, even.

"Be sure and get some cake. I think they're going to cut it soon."

Cate did not respond for a moment, but then she smiled carefully, and nodded him by as he passed her to join his family.

Joshua Hamilton

Joshua Hamilton is a Louisville, KY native who migrated to Corpus Christi, TX with his family. Between Kentucky and Texas, he has traveled and lived in several places, including Spain, Appalachia, Panamá, Peru, the Philippines, and the Colorado River. He teaches Spanish at TAMUCC, has published a chapbook, Slow Wind, with Finishing Line Press, and has poems appearing in or forthcoming from Driftwood Press and Windward Review.

Mulch

Desiccate splintered forest
ground up and spat out
under the feet - accumulated
bits of growth, decay, sunlight worded into leaves
and chainsaws articulated
into kindling - like
the devastation of a bad life
ground up and strewn
in an attempt to soften
the inevitable crash
landing.

Signal Path

Cars through a fine morning mist
set an expectant rhythm;
their percussive conductors
bend silhouettes
over steering wheels, into an explosion
of day.
Ingrained behavior
amplifies addictive nature
into a bass note
thrumming deep from dirt crust,
then trebling out through the fx pedals
of cities
and suburbs.
But the sweet chintzy mist
and relaxing drone
                        bark and root
along the floodplain
for a brief moment play counterpoint
to the human music crescendo,
pulling it down,
and closer
to an unconstructed
chthonic
harmony.

Illusion of Movement

Like succubi, except that felines
stalk dreams with dumb
hectic furnaces of thought
(hunger, stimulus, nothing).
Their vibrating temperatures
both suck the energy from every room
and signify its great
expenditure.
Whiskery thermometers
and temperamental
surveillance:
parallels
to our naval-minded thought,
so that when you and I
move past that fork in the road,
we still get stuck on our tines,
roasting
in a hectic furnace.

Tools for Feeding the Flood

In the dark stutter of night
hours flash from small displays,
nervous fingers wake up devices
that sleep in sixty seconds.

Outside, ancient rustles
sift down through oak leaves
and maple branches,
stir empty streets into morning gravity.

Chronology of turf arranges human force
towards chthonic flows of noon and midnight
destructions that melt, while we work and
sleep, distracted, old sign systems.

Moving through manicured yards
and those strewn with toys and bare dirt,
pulverizing multitudes of histories gathered
in antique stores, piled in junk shops,

yawn and groan of inhuman earth
tide-plows through amber
and copper-green patinas, lit submarine blue,
history and invention sucked down:

fragments of wicker chairs, rotary phones,
typewriters, die-punches, porcelain-ware,
until emptied out into the river
below town — hodge-podge

play-doh grenade of meaning and object
rising but not breaking the surface —
ghostly inundation with hinges rusted open
scooping the slow current in its trajectory.

Notecards on the Abandonment

[A]guas azules: Notecard #11

> *"Plumas de saliva las escamas*
> *Perfectas del alcohol"*
> —José María Álvarez

> *"Hé would be prepared to líve in a world of Fall*
> *for ever"*
> —John Berryman

In southern Mexico
footpaths trickle
onto palatial nudity of waters
bluer that the passing
of beach-drunk sky

[R]ighteous: Notecard #13

Righteous ferries the long soul
across palisaded convection of light—
thin river made wide and tattle of mosquito
orchestrates the inner chambers (flaw in the silence).
Fanfare. Small wave / long wave.
Isolated blades of logic, green delicates,
will hold balanced evening's bipolarity
when the shore comes, shores up irresolution
in generous deserts of gray, of nothing, of this
we're sure.

[T]own of Bedrock: Notecard #18

> *"Sabéis*
> *que nuestras verdades son voluntariosas,*
> *lo mismo que el arbusto*
> *tenaz en la roca salobre,*
> *hundiendo sus raíces*

> *en un poco de arena*
> *terrosa, entre dos piedras*
> *que se separarán."*
> —Carlos Barral

Voluntary truth
crumbling at rock root:
Wilma's invariables—her world broken loose,
Dino vagrant with almost purpose,
Fred tumbled to a has-been-bottom
with his empty bottles hidden
among bed strewn limbs and pebbles.
But this stone wife in repose
knows the quarry provides, waits
for the next instant reinvention wheel.

[D]ismembered Ritual: Notecard #12

Exit, arms stretching, balcony right—
clotted morning of boom clouds flushes
lightning down a collapsing stairwell—
sudden and crackling destiny lines
scraped across the palm!
Million sappy trees green strong and horizon,
but these underfoot: hacked, dried,
rough humanned from their intimate cycles—
a pattering firmament holding no longer.

[E]xpectation: Notecard #28

When hair grows long
and seasons with it
put away clippers and comb—
let wind and stillness
arrange everything.

Lee Hultin

Lee Hultin found success in writing technical manuals from plumbing to technology that led her to a career in application development. After retiring early and looking for new adventures, she left Chicago's cold winters and settled on the Island. These days, she spends her time enjoying island life on the Gulf with her rescued husky mix and writing about life.

It's Five O'Clock Somewhere

  I woke in the dark room. All the doors were closed, the drapes and blinds drawn tight. Jack didn't like the sun waking him. He lay still sleeping by my side. I couldn't sleep anymore and I had to see the sun, the light, the Gulf. I decided I wasn't going to waste any more time waiting on Jack.
  Outside, Marty was tinkering on the boat. It was red with white cushions, and his pride and joy. He had just traded up, his older boat for the used red one. It was bigger and more powerful than the old one, and seated eight, a definite boost over the four-seater older one. He had only logged a month on it and was still getting used to how it performed. He was having problems with the GPS working properly and a few minor issues with the motor.
  Inside, I helped Jessica put the beer in the tote along with chips and nuts. "Let's get going," Marty said as he entered the sliding glass doors. Jack emerged finally, freshly showered and grabbed a cold beer. Jessica laughed and said, "A bit early isn't it Jack." Jack just smiled and said, "It's five o'clock somewhere," letting out a not so quiet belch while walking down to the pier. I grabbed my sunglasses, hat and hairclip, taking the tote on the way out the door. Jessica locked the lanai doors and walked the 15 steps to the boat. Marty was already in the boat yelling at Jessica, "Did you bring my sunglasses?" "Right here" she said, handing them to him. With everyone on board, Marty turned the motor on and backed out of the pier, put the boat in gear and drove slowly down

the canal.

I never tired of the slow crawl moving past beautiful houses, looking at the landscape and imagining living in one. Some still had their hurricane shutters up, meaning it was a second home. I wondered what these people did for a living to have more than one house. They had perfectly manicured lawns with foliage discreetly hiding patios and swimming pools, jet skis and large boats in private piers, and they were so much bigger than my own house. Jessica remarked on a red, garden pagoda in one yard on the corner lot to the Intracoastal. "That's new," she said. "The couple who bought that house also owns a new Asian restaurant on Water Street." Jessica always knew when something changed or who was home or who had bought or sold these beautiful homes.

Marty opened it up, and the little red boat was flying, the engine purring loudly. Three dolphins, attracted by the engine sound and the bubbles the large wake created, were following us. Soon they were jumping alongside, greeting us on this mostly cloudless day. I pulled my hair back and secured it at the nape of my neck with a large clip.

Marty turned right, slowing as he came to little patches of sand islands. They really weren't islands, only what was left of sand bars moved by the sea and tide. It was the long way around the Island to the Gulf. Marty had said earlier we would stay close to shore since the forecast predicted a few storms. I didn't mind, I loved being in the boat and taking a little journey around the Island.

Soon we were into the Gulf with the Island on our right. You couldn't stay too close to the Island because of shallow waters and unexpected sand bars, so Marty moved a bit further out, still keeping the Island in sight. I moved upfront sitting beside him and opened the windshield windows. I loved putting my feet up and feeling the boat bouncing off the waves. The wind picked up and the waves were now becoming swells rising higher and higher on both sides of the red boat. I was laughing at each jump the boat made over the waves, coming down hard on the sea. Thrilled by the roller-coaster ride, my laughter got louder as the adrenaline pulsed in my veins. I looked back at Jack and smiled. He acknowledged me by raising a can of beer. He only liked sitting up front when the waters were smooth as glass.

To the west, we all saw it. Dark skies were rapidly moving

east and in our direction. Marty sped up and Jack started to get nervous and said so. Jessica and I switched seats so she could help navigate and I sat beside Jack. Jessica was trying to get the GPS on her cell phone to work. "Let's get back Marty. I don't like the looks of that storm coming in," she said calmly. Before she even finished her sentence fog appeared seemingly out of nowhere. I looked at Jack, a silly grin on his face, taking a sip from another can of beer. In seconds the fog covered the red boat and we could only see a couple of feet in front of us. Jack exploded, "Were all going to die." I chuckled, "I fully trust Marty, and I think we are in capable hands. After all, Marty knows these waters and has been driving in the Gulf for over 15 years." Jack's face, reddened by the coastal sun from our few days of vacation, was now pale. He gripped the bar around the side of the red motorboat with one hand, his knuckles as white as his face, while keeping his other hand firmly around the beer can. "Marty, I don't want to crash or die," Jack voiced in a hoarse whisper.

I could see the side of Marty's face: it was as pale as Jack's. He said softly, "I'm not sure where we are. I don't know if we are close to the Island anymore." The swells and wind were lifting the boat in the air. We hit the water with a hard slap that shook the boat and lifted us from our seats. The fog was so thick I couldn't see beyond the edge of the boat. Only then did I begin to wonder if maybe, just maybe we might be in trouble.

Bob James

Bob James is a native of the Chicago area, growing up in Oak Park, Ill. He currently lives in Corpus Christi, TX. He recently retired after 25 years in the education business – one year as a sign language interpreter followed by 24 years as a teacher in the fields of Special Education and Technology. All of his work can be accessed through his new site, Bob James – The Author. He writes daily devotionals, Science Fiction and Thrillers, and is also working on a book about the journey that he and his wife went through during her battle with breast cancer. Bob has been married to his wife Lucy since 1979. They have two sons, one daughter, one granddaughter, and one grandson.

One Last Performance

Jason Riordan looked at himself in the mirror, using an eyeliner pencil to make the last adjustments to his makeup. He had to support his right hand with his left to quell the shaking. "That'll work," he said out loud, even though no one could hear him. He still had a private dressing room, in deference to his past greatness. He might not have the starring roles anymore. He might make more mistakes in his lines, but he still commanded the respect of audiences and directors because of his reputation and his perseverance in the face of Parkinson's. There was a knock on the door. "Ten minutes, Mr. Riordan," the assistant to the assistant director called as he opened the door just a crack to deliver his message. Jason smiled. His timing on getting his makeup done was still perfect. Ever since he'd started in theater, he had done his own makeup. "It helps me as I become my character," he had told countless makeup artists. And now, his routine to get into character would continue. He stared at the mirror, inspecting his makeup one last time. Satisfied, he slowly closed his eyes and went over the play in his mind. He muttered softly, reciting his lines, and telling himself where to make his entrances.

He wanted this performance to be perfect and got so wrapped up in his preparation that he realized he must have missed the underling's five-minute call. As the first notes of the overture sounded, he cursed silently. His routine called for him to be ready in the wings before the overture started playing. Now, he rushed to get to his place, so he could take his centering breaths a few seconds before his entrance. His first starring role ever was with this director as "George" in Our Town and now, knowing Jason's condition, this same director had made a special accommodation to allow him to begin this version of Our Town, as the Stage Manager, with the freedom to look back on his career and give the audience a chance to acknowledge their appreciation for the retiring actor. They had flocked to see the once-great Jason Riordan in his last performance. Those who had acted alongside him including the first Emily and Stage Manager were in the audience, actors who had worked with him in the performances that had earned him his Tony nominations, and various assorted fans who wanted to pay their respects to one who, even in his ongoing illness, showed grace and respect to his fans. He got to his spot on the wing with a little over a minute to spare, and he took a couple of cool-down breaths. Then, he did that which he had never done before in his career, he pulled back the curtain and peeked at the audience. The stage lights kept him from seeing much, but the memories he had made with those people he saw and recognized overwhelmed him and left him with a slight case of stage fright. He closed the curtain and took another deep breath, and then, he was on. From that first, special monologue to his final line, he was perfect. He didn't suffer from the dropped lines or cues that had plagued him in recent years. His swan song performance was amazing, and the audience recognized it. Decorum was thrown to the winds as his fans screamed his name and he took bow after bow. The stage hands picked up flowers that were thrown in congratulations. He left the stage triumphantly after one of his finest performances ever. He walked back to his dressing room accepting handshakes, hugs, and pats on the backs from the cast and crew. He kept looking at the floor, lest they see his tears. He arrived at his dressing room and lay his head on the makeup table to rest for a few minutes before taking his makeup off one last time. He didn't want to take it off just yet, because that would make his retirement final.

****

The assistant to the assistant director knocked on Mr. Riordan's door. "Five minutes, until you go on Mr. Riordan," he said, opening the door just a crack to deliver his message. He waited for the customary acknowledgment. There was none. He knocked harder and called out louder. When he got no answer, he ran in and saw Jason Riordan slumped with his head down on the makeup table. He checked for a pulse. When he didn't get a pulse, he ran out in the hall and looked for a stage hand. "Get the director!" he yelled.

***

"That is how you found him?" the director asked, trying to find a pulse. He teared up a little when he realized that Riordan was gone. He walked behind the body to get to the other side and looked at his face. He wiped away his tears and smiled himself when he saw Riordan's smile. It was that shy, after-performance smile that he used when he'd look at the director and ask how he'd done. "It would have been one, great, last performance," he said as he closed Riordan's eyes.

Allyson Chavez Larkin

Allyson Chavez Larkin is a family physician specializing in wound care. She lives in Corpus Christi, Texas with her unfailingly patient husband, a Midwest transplant who still cannot get used to the heat, and three lovely children who are turning into amazing people right in front of her eyes. She reads and writes voraciously in her spare time. Middle grade and young adult fiction are her guilty pleasures.

Jesus Lopez Mows His Lawn

Jesus Lopez mows his own lawn. So do I of course. So do most of us; but Mr. Lopez is paraplegic.

Twenty-five years ago, a bullet lodged in Jesus Lopez's back severing the neurologic connection between his spine and legs. Now no signal reaches the muscles below his waist. Paralysis and deformity ensued. His feet are contracted and twisted upside down so that they look like curved bowls -- no good for walking or even standing for that matter. So, Mr. Lopez mows his yard in his wheelchair.

****

Mr. Lopez's home health nurse keeps calling me, complaining that his dressings are dirty or have fallen off when she goes out to care for him three times a week. She can't figure out why. So this visit I've got to have a "heart to heart" with him about his role in the healing process.

"Mr. Lopez, you won't heal unless you are compliant with our wound care plan. If your dressings are dirty or wet when the home nurse sees you, you will never heal."

"Sorry Doctora." That is what he calls me. "I think it might be the mowing. I'll tie a grocery bag on my foot from now on to keep the bandage clean."

"Mowing? How do you manage that?"

"I pull my chair right up next to the mower so I can pull the crank at the same time I squeeze the start paddle on the handle."

"It's a push mower?" I cannot believe what I am hearing.

"You bet, self-propelled. Once I get it started, the mowing is easy."

I shake my head.

"I pull my chair up behind the mower and push it with my left hand. I drive the wheelchair with my right."

"That doesn't sound safe," I say as I inspect the horseshoe-shaped ulcer on top of his right foot, which due to his contractures, is actually resting on the footplate of his wheelchair.

"I tie that belt around my legs to keep them from flopping if I hit a rut." Mr. Lopez points to a frayed brown leather belt draped on the edge of his seat. A jagged tear in the cushion has been repaired with silver duct tape and a shopping bag chock full of gear -- a sack lunch, an umbrella, a blanket -- hangs off the handles. "I've never had a bit of trouble."

The wound is pink and shallow. It looks like it should heal right up; but never does. It is maddening. "Dirt and debris getting into your dressing isn't doing your foot much good either," I say.

"I have to do it, Doctora. I have a big yard and if I don't keep it cut, the city will fine me $75. I'm not made of money."

That's true. He gets to my office by bus, but unlike a lot of my bus patients, he is never late. I should have Mr. Lopez give a class: "How to Master Public Transportation and Arrive On Time." I didn't even know he took the bus until one day I ran so late that I made him miss the last pick-up. He had to borrow the phone at the front desk to shift around for someone to pick him up.

****

"Jesus Lopez's mother died," my medical assistant warns me before I go in for our next visit.

"I'm so sorry, Mr. Lopez," I say as I look at his foot.

"Thank you Doctora. I miss her. We were very close, but she was old. It was her time."

"You lived with her?"

"Yes, just her and I. The house is very quiet now."

"How are you managing? Have you had to move?"

"Doctora," Mr. Lopez pauses waiting until I look up and give him my full attention. "My mother couldn't get out of bed this last year. I managed to take care of her. I sure can take care of myself."

I blush. This is the closest to an angry word I have ever had from Mr. Lopez, and I deserve every bit of it. I've been treating him for a year, but I don't understand a thing about his life.

"I'm so sorry. I didn't mean -- I just assumed." I struggled for words. I did not want to offend this man, always so courteous and patient. "But how do you possibly manage? It's not just your paralysis, but your feet. You can't even -- "

"Doctora. I got shot over twenty years ago -- and it was pretty much my own fault. For a few weeks I thought all about 'I can't.' I couldn't get out of my mind all the things I would never do. But then I decided, 'Hey, I'm alive. The Lord is not done with me.' So, every day I just do everything I can do."

I am humbled and have no response.

"So I took care of my mother. I owed her that. She gave me life and I wasn't gonna put her in a nursing home."

"You're like MacGyver," I say.

"Oh Doctora," Mr. Lopez laughs, "I love that show."

I have an idea. "Do you think if I put home health on hold, you can figure out how to you reach down to your foot and dress the wound yourself everyday?"

"I'll find a way if you tell me what I need to do."

****

"Jesus Lopez is healed." My medical assistant moon walks in the hall outside Mr. Lopez's room at his follow up appointment two weeks later.

I walk into the room, hoping but not convinced. I shine the spotlight on his foot. Indeed there is a thin, translucent layer of pink tissue over the wound.

"Mr. Lopez, you are healed." I can't help but grin.

"I thought you'd like that, Doctora. Thank you for healing me."

"Mr. Lopez, are you kidding? You did it. I'm just sorry I didn't have you change your own dressings months ago."

"That's OK, Doctora. You always did your best. Sometimes it takes trying different things before you get them right."

Skoot Larson

Skoot Larson is a native Los Angelino, a musician, music critic and a Viet Nam veteran. He has also worked as a disc jockey, actor, speech therapist, stand-up comedian, behavioral counselor and streetcar conductor. His previous works include the Lars Lindstrom Zen-Jazz Mystery series, a black-humor novel about health care in America entitled "Apollo Issue," and a political humor novel, "The Palestine Solution," the King Irv fantasy series, and The Dave Holman Texas Detective mysteries. Skoot lives with his two cats, Miles and Dexter, in Rockport, Texas.

The Three Little 21st Century Pigs

Once upon a harvest moon, there were three little pigs; A very conservative Fox News kinda pig, a moderate, middle-class type conformist pig, and a wigged-out, very vouty cool and free-thinking pig.

The first little pig was too lazy to build a house of his own. He bitched that the government wasn't setting him up for an inexpensive place to crash and finally bought a clapped-out old single-wide mobile home in the woods, landscaped with worn rotting tires and discarded, rusting appliances.

The conformist second little pig bought a three-bedroom, two bath pad in a Levitt Town tract where all the houses looked so much alike he had to count the doors every night coming home to make sure he was walking into the right crib.

The very vouty third little pig built himself a mad pad on the beach out of baritone sax reeds and palm fronds with a hip little bar and multiple hammocks swingin' free!

As the little pigs were settling into their Texas coastal life, a big bad wolf hitch hikin' down with the snowbirds from Minnesota stopped off feelin' hungry and unfulfilled. Unfamiliar with the territory, the big bad wolf cut east from the highway and started makin' tracks through the dark circuitous oaken woods. After a long bit of a trapes, the wolf found himself in a ghetto-looking clearing filled with rusting junk, rotting tires and a big aluminum box covered with Kudzu vines, Texas flags and No Trespassing signs. The wolf approached cautiously, mounted the three rotting wood steps and applied his hairy knuckles to the rusting screen door.

"Who goes there?" thundered the frightened but macho pig. "Don't you know you're standin' on private property? You'd better not be a Jehovah's Witless or something, or I'll blow you away!"

"It's cool," shouted the wolf. "I'm just here to check your meters."

When the up-tight pig opened the door, the big bad wolf gave him a wide, saliva-dripping grin. "You look like a tasty pork morsel," the canine creature told him. "I think I'll huff and I'll puff and I'll blow your joint down... Then I'll have me a sort of Cajon pork sandwich with extra jalapeños!"

The red-neck pig called for his kids to fetch him his shotgun, but the over-zealous pig kids came out too fast, tripping and letting loose with a blast that sent their daddy to that big pig sty in the sky.

Not wanting to be on the scene when the gendarmerie arrived, the big bad wolf legged it east toward the coast. After a long trot through the forest, the big bad wolf came on a tract of poorly constructed houses. Hoping to blend in with the low budget surroundings, the wolf strolled down the main drag, selecting a non-descript pad with a cheap Korean car in the drive and walking up to the door with a wolfish grin. He sounded the bell and hung back until a nervous little pig opened the door.

"I always try to be politically correct," said the pig that answered the door. "But your presence here could be bringin' down the property values. What do you want, and make it quick, before my neighbors see you here and think I'm a bleeding heart liberal or something!"

"I'll come right to the point," the wolf told him. "I'm starvin', Marvin and I need a little roast pork. So I'm gonna huff and puff and blow your square little house down, and then I'll make a three course meal of you and your piggy kin!"

The second little pig came on like a Kung-Fu master, layin' all the moves he learned in self-defense class on the unsuspecting wolf. The wolf blew the pig's house down, but not before the very square pig landed a shot in his wedding tackle and sent him off in great pain.

Limping east across the wet flood plain, the big bad wolf soon arrived at the beach, where he saw a smart little Tiki Hut near the water's edge. Approaching cautiously, the big bad wolf circled the structure, sniffing the air for wolf traps. His olfactory senses were quickly filled with the scent of illegal weed and Patchouli oil. Hesitantly, the wolf raised his knuckles and laid a crisp paradiddle on the thin reed door.

A little pig in shades and a black beret answered his call. "Welcome my brother," the porcine cat greeted him. "Glad you could fall on by!"

"Porque, Porky," the wolf responded, "Ain't you afraid of me?"

"Like, should I be?" the hip little pig questioned. "We're all God's children in this veil of tears."

"But," responded the wolf, "I intend to huff and puff and to blow your house down!"

"Crazy!" cried the cool pig. "Like I got an old tenor sax in here somewhere…"

"What about a reed?" queried the wolf without thinking.

"Are you kidding?" said the pig. "The whole house is made of reeds. Just pull one out and trim it down!"

"But I'm here to eat you up!" shouted the pig.

"Oh man," said the pig with a serious face, "Don't you know how bad pork is for you? It's a genuine life shortener! Clog your arteries and give you those triggie-whatsis worms… Man, like this pork isn't even organic!"

"I can dig that," said the wolf, "But like I'm two days short of three squares!"

"No worries," answered the pig, "we'll send out for a pizza while we jam!"

"Too much!" said the big bad wolf. "Can we get extra anchovies?"

"If you can huff and puff like Prez," the cool little pig told him, "You can have anything you want on it… Except pork…"

"Oh man," the wolf told him. "Bacon was never really my thing anyway. Do you know Cool Blues in E-flat?"

Carol Mays

Carol Mays wrote 103 Crazy Ideas for Surviving Suburbia. She also co-wrote Escape from Sunny Shores with her husband, William. She is currently working on a novel about Nevins, a cat who adopts a homeless boy.

Pepper Cane's Rant
(A Humorous Christmas Story for Adults)

    Merry Christmas, you say? For you maybe, but not for me! I mean, who ever heard of one of Santa's elves getting arrested and having to do community service? That's the mess I'm in now! You see, I'm an elf -- a real elf -- who just so happens to have made one little mistake and now I'm sentenced to 60 hours of community service during the Christmas season at this stupid mall as -- get this -- are you ready? An elf -- helping the imposter Santa at the Picture Gallery. It's a mind numbing nightmare. On top of my 60 hours, I have to go to anger management sessions with this complete idiot -- some psychologist, named Dr. Phil. He kinda looks like the Grinch with his bald head and beady eyes. And, really I shouldn't be here. The mall, I mean. It's kinda all your fault -- well, maybe not yours but people like you. You see, most people think elves live at the North Pole, are short, eat tons of sweets and make toys all day long. WRONG!!!!!

    Elves are everywhere doing all sorts of jobs -- not just toy making and baking. I don't have tons of time to explain this to you but let me see if I can. There are two kinds of elves: Green Hats and Red Hats. Green Hat elves are construction workers, plumbers, electricians, you know -- skilled labor stuff. At the North Pole they do the baking, card making and any sled repairs needed. Red Hat elves, which is what I am, make toys at the North Pole, and are often teachers, doctors, nurses, writers and stuff like that everywhere else. I used to be a top Red Hat Elf before the Incident. I made simple things which kids used to want for Christmas:

blankets, pillows, stuffed toys, and my best of all: Sock Monkey. That's been popular for a long time until that bitch stole it from me and mass-produced Sock Monkey -- and not very well made I might add. I found out about it when Spike -- oh, you don't know him. Do you? You might. He's a Red Hat hot-looking elf with spiked blue hair, edible piercings, and a tattoo of a red hat on his right arm. Well, Spike makes wild, cool, crazy cool toys that do amazing things. He invented pop rocks, exploding volcanos, motorized scooters just for kids, well just about anything that explodes or flies. He's so cool. Well, Spike is the one who told me that Candy Land -- the bitch -- stole my Sock Monkey and changed the look to get away with it. She thinks she is so wonderful just because she's from the wealthy and famous family who invented the game -- Candy Land. She's used to getting her own way and when -- oh, yeah she's a Red Hat elf too if I failed to mention that but I guess you could've figure that out. Oh, where was I? I get so mad I forget what I'm talking about. Oh, yeah. She stole my pattern of Sock Monkey off my desk and instead of him being the usual brown sock she made all different variations of Sock Monkey -- that part was fine -- all she had to do was ask me. But the part that is not o.k. is that she makes them talk and say some nauseating, high pitch-voiced phrases that when you pull the string it makes a: pooshk sound and says, -- "Candy Land is my favorite game! Pooshk -- Candy Land is where I want to live! Pooshk -- Candy Land is fun for you and me!" It's selling at an over-priced store ironically at this stupid mall.

Well, I got so mad that I confronted her at one of our Christmas parties. It was such a perfect party too. Chocolate fountain, pizza, a crystal ball and rock- n -roll Christmas music. Spike was playing the electric guitar and singing. Oh, he's so hot!

"Candy!" I yelled. "What the hell do you think you're doing stealing my Sock Monkey and making it your own?" She turned and looked at me with her perfect grape eyes -- all the guy elves love purple-grape eyes -- I have chocolate-brown eyes but you can see that -- and in her annoying fake-whisper sweet voice she had the nerve to say, "I don't know what you are talking about. I checked and your Sock Monkey didn't have your name on it. You didn't register it. So, I just perfected it and made it more up-to-date and cool. Oh, and my Sock Monkey -- registered in my name -- has accessories. So, I don't know what you're talking about

Peppercane." She patted me on the head -- because she's taller than me. I snapped. I completely lost it. On her. I never lost it like I did at that party. I can remember Spike yelling, "Way cool! An elf chick fight!" I kicked her knees then, I punched her face making her red velvet Louis Vuitton Hat sail across the room and land at Santa's feet. Candy's eyes rolled back, then she hit the floor with a wobbly thud. Santa looked at me with a grave expression.

You can guess the rest. Rudolf couldn't keep a secret if his red nose and Christmas depended on it. I was arrested, booked and put in a cell across from the real Grinch -- not Dr. Phil. There were some others there on the naughty list. I can't believe I just snapped like that. I really can't explain myself. I've been taking it from her all my life and I just couldn't take it anymore. Dr. Phil says I'm a disgruntled elf and says I should, "just let thangs go -- invent somethin' new and register your inventions from now on." I wanted to punch him when he said that, but I just smiled and said, "Thank you, I will do that from now on. I am so fortunate to have your help." Santa bailed me out and is giving me a second chance.

Well, I guess I better get back to work my break is almost over. I see a long line of kids waiting to tell the fake Santa what they want for Christmas. I hope it's not Candy's stupid talking Sock Monkey. Wait -- I'm getting a text. It's from Spike! He's asking me to the annual Christmas Ball! I guess it's a Merry Christmas after all!

William Mays

William Mays has written Family Obligations, a mob novel. He also co-wrote Escape from Sunny Shores with his wife Carol. In addition he has published a book of nature photos, The View from Oso Creek. He is currently working on "George, The Lost Middle Years," a dark comedy about the sex, drugs, and rock-and-roll era of the 1970s.

Judgment Day

Sam, feeling more desperately bored than normal, scanned the long curving rows of the stadium. He hoped to see something new, something different. No luck. Above and below, to his left and right, the rows, all crowded with people, stretched as far as he could see, seemingly to infinity, blurring together at the extremities.

In front of him there was nothing. The other side of the stadium - if there was another side - was too far away to be seen. The sky - if it was sky - was clear, not blue or hazy or cloudy, nor was there a breeze or a smell.

"Maybe we should start again?" he asked Chen.

Chen sat next to him. They had recounted their lives to each other many times in great detail. That was the only way to beat back the ruthless monotony, but they had told the stories so many times that they were no longer interesting. There were things Sam hadn't divulged, things he didn't want to admit. His life hadn't been perfect. Whose life had? Why should he talk about the bad stuff?

After what might have been hours, Chen answered. "There is something I've never mentioned." He spoke only Mandarin, but it sounded like English to Sam. Likewise, Sam spoke only English, but it sounded like Mandarin to Chen. "An American movie. Dirty Harry. My wife and I went to see it a theater."

Sam had seen that movie too. It was one of those things he didn't want to mention.

"I was starting my own business when I saw it," Chen said, his voice trembling.

Sam too had seen it when he was starting his business. He and Chen had been born at almost exactly the same time, married at the same time, and both their wives had died of cancer at about the same time. Sam had always assumed there was some reason the two of them had wound up next to each other, and perhaps the reason was about to be revealed.

An angel interrupted them. It appeared to their left. Merely a white blip at first, it drifted steadily in their direction. They flew by every so often, but Sam had no idea how often. There was no night or day, no sun or moon, no change whatsoever, nothing by which to gauge time.

Everyone in their row and the adjoining rows, turned to watch. What else was there to do in the stadium?

This one looked like a boy, clean-shaven, soft, but with a defined jaw, wide mouth, and pronounced cheekbones. Did that mean something? It slowed as it neared them. Was it his time for some final, horrible judgement? Or Chen's? How would he ever pass the time without Chen?

It stopped in front of the woman on Sam's right. She and Sam had never spoken. She talked only to the man to her right. They spoke a language like nothing Sam had ever heard with lots of clicking and popping sounds, like insects. She was black with short-cropped hair, rather young-looking, and he was old and tall with pale skin. The angel pointed its finger at her. She screamed and tried to escape, but that was impossible. No one could leave.

Her clicking became frantic. She grabbed for the pale man, and he reached for her. Their fingers came close, but never quite touched. She chattered to him, and he responded, and then she was gone. No cloud of smoke, no poof, no sound. Simply gone. And there was a man in her place. He was old and wrinkled, and he and the pale man talked in that annoying clicking language. It was as if they had known each other forever. The memory of the woman slipped from Sam's brain. He tried to retain it, pressing his eyes tight shut, visualizing her face. The image slipped away, though. He opened his eyes, not remembering why he had shut them. The old, wrinkled man and the tall, pale man were talking, as they always had.

More time passed. Hours? Days?

"I guess we have to talk about the movie," Sam said. "I loved it because I thought of myself like Harry, a tough guy who got things done. I can remember that night as clear as anything in my life. I'd had a fight with my wife. She wasn't even my wife yet. It looked like we were going to break up. I didn't want to marry her. But her father had offered to help me in my business, and I felt I would never be a success without him. So, I called her, and we went to the movie, and got married a few months later."

Chen shuddered "That's exactly the way it worked for me. I didn't want to marry my wife, but her father would help me with my business. I called her up, and we went to the movie, and got married a few months later."

"We saw it on Christmas Day," Sam said. "We went to the last showing. At ten at night."

"We saw it the day after Christmas. At eleven in the morning." He got a funny look on his face. "With the time zone differences between us, that means --."

"-- we saw it at exactly the same time!" they said in unison.

An angel moved steadily toward them. The face was clearly defined. A young woman. Yes, it was her. What he had feared. He had been trying to remember her name ever since he died, but he couldn't.

She pointed at him, and he found himself floating alone in a blue ether. A blinding light hurt his eyes, yet the pain was almost welcome since it was the first thing he had felt since he died.

"Sam," a Voice called out to him. It came from no particular place. It might have even been coming from inside his head. Was this the time of Judgement? The Voice didn't sound God-like though. It was a bit nasally, and had a rather pronounced Texas drawl. And there was a lot of background noise. People talking, phones ringing. Like a boiler room.

Sam put his hand up to shield his eyes. "Where am I? Is this hell? Purgatory?"

"Do you think you could explain algebra to a cockroach?"

"No, I couldn't do that."

The bedroom of his house materialized. It looked the way it had early in their marriage. His wife came into the room, her white bathrobe around her. She was young, and he was struck by her beauty, so unlike the bitter drunk she became.

"I will not go to the party," she screamed.

He too looked young, virile, and handsome. "You will go."

"No, I will not! I will not pretend anymore. Never again."

"Be quiet. The children will hear. The neighbors will hear."

Her voice grew louder. "I don't care who hears!"

He grabbed her by the collar and slapped her. "Shut up."

She started crying.

He slapped her on the other cheek. "If you don't go, I will divorce you. I don't need you or your father anymore. Don't disobey me. You will regret it."

The fight drained out of her as she sank onto the bed. He still held onto her collar. The sash came undone and the robe slipped loose.

What pleasure to dominate and destroy a human being. It's what he had lived for. Like the time he demolished his boyhood friend. His office materialized around him.

"It was my idea, Sam!" his friend yelled. "You stole it from me. You're going to make a fortune. I deserve a share. There's enough for both of us."

It wouldn't have hurt Sam to toss a few crumbs to his friend. But what fun would that be? "You get a paycheck. Take it or leave it."

His friend turned red in the face. "From the beginning everything was my idea."

The greatest pleasure came from stringing the con out as long as possible, so Sam decided to play one more trick on him. "Sure, I'll take care of you. Don't worry."

The fool believed his lie. As soon as he left, Sam called the police and said his friend had threatened to kill him. What pleasure when they came and arrested him and everyone stared. He had destroyed two human beings. Well three, counting the young woman whose name he still couldn't remember.

The office disappeared and Sam floated in the ether. He felt the warmth of the sun. The light dimmed to the reddish shade of a sunset. The pleasing aroma of the sea filled the ether. A cool sea breeze caressed his face. Then a foul smell, like rotting fish, floated in on the breeze, the stench growing worse and worse, waves of nausea overtaking his body. He'd never experienced anything so miserable. The boredom of the stadium would have been better.

The nausea stopped.

"Have you had time to contemplate your actions?" the Voice asked.

Did his entry into heaven depend on the right answers? He'd always been good at bullshit. "Yes, I have, and I decided I was a sinner."

"So, you are repenting?"

"Yes, I am."

He was in the back seat of the car with the young woman, but he still couldn't remember her name. He lied to her, of course. Told her he'd help her if she got pregnant. Told her she could trust him. And she believed him. What ecstasy to con someone so completely.

Eight and a half months later, on Christmas Day, he and his wife-to-be were at the movie theater, standing in line to buy popcorn. The young woman appeared at the end of the line. She was pregnant, very pregnant. When she saw him, she wobbled on her feet and fainted. Sam paid for the food and raced away, yet he couldn't help looking back for one last pleasurable gaze at her on the floor.

The vision faded.

"Sometimes things are set in motion," the Voice said. There was loud music in the background. And laughter. Were they having a party? Someone was singing "All My Exes Live in Texas" in a really bad voice. Was it Karaoke night in Heaven?

"You can't blame me for being strong. For being aggressive. For doing what I had to do to survive."

The pleasing aroma of the sea filled the ether. The light dimmed to a reddish shade. Waves gently crashed into shore. Gulls cawed. His skin tingled as unseen fingers moved across his back and chest. A woman was massaging him. He couldn't see her, but her breath was hot on his cheek. Then, he felt the stubble of a beard. It was a man! The fingers became knives, cutting him over and over, going deeper and deeper. He screamed, expected to see blood all over his body, but there was nothing, not even marks on his skin. The knives became burning hot pokers. Flames engulfed him, choking smoke clogged his lungs. Surely, he was in hell.

When the pain finally subsided, there was nothing. Endless time, and no way to count it. He started telling the story of his life to himself, as if he were talking to Chen. He included all the omitted scenes. Then he started telling himself Chen's stories. He had heard them so many times it was if they were his stories. A funny thing happened. He began including scenes Chen had omitted, scenes Sam had no way of knowing anything about. They were nearly identical to Sam's omitted scenes. What was going on?

"One more thing to show you," the Voice said.

"What is this? A Christmas Carol?"

"Is that a made-for-TV movie?"

A teenage girl appeared in front of him.

"That is your daughter, Sam."

She walked down a dark alley in a rundown neighborhood. Two-story brownstones lined both sides. A garbage can had fallen over and rats were eating the contents. She stepped around them and followed an emaciated man with scraggly, long hair up a long, narrow staircase to a room where people were shooting up drugs. When she shot up, her eyes rolled up in their sockets, and she collapsed.

"What's wrong?" Sam asked, panicked.

"Your daughter died at the age of eighteen from a drug overdose."

He started crying. "That's horrible."

"You don't know how horrible. She was a brilliant young girl. The algorithms indicate that with even a little child support from you, she would not have fallen prey to drugs. She would have become the President of the United States. She would have brokered true peace in the Middle East, and presided over a period of unprecedented world prosperity. She would have been considered the best President in American history."

"What can I do to make things right? I'll do anything. Give me a chance."

"It doesn't work that way. The algorithms are inflexible. It's all mathematics."

"So what's going to happen to me?"

"Hard to say. There are a lot of irrational numbers, expansions that neither terminate nor become periodic."

Sam didn't understand at all, but suddenly he found himself back in the stadium again next to Chen, and he didn't care anymore. He couldn't wait to once again tell the story of his life, except this time it would be a different story. He thought of all the things he wished he'd done or said, all the missed possibilities. He would invent the ideal life, including the story about his daughter who became President. He could change it around each time he told it, adding scenes, deleting scenes. That would make it endlessly interesting. He was happy for the first time since he died.

"Hello Chen, how are you?"

Chen responded with lots of clicking and popping sounds, more like the sounds an insect would make than a human. Sam screamed so loud that even the people five and six rows up turned to look. He kept screaming, his voice never getting hoarse. Finally, though, he grew bored with the screaming and sat silent.

Jim McCutchon

Dr. Jim McCutchon practiced medicine in Corpus Christi for many years before retiring to pursue other interests, one of which is writing. He is currently working on a novel about life on a 19th century plantation in Louisiana. As an exercise while studying the writing craft at a workshop in Santa Barbara California, he was challenged by the moderator to write a short story containing a very specific ending, and to do it in ten minutes. The following is that story.

Emergency

He was sitting at his desk after lunch, talking with three associates. An important business meeting. He had left strict instructions—no calls, no interruptions of any kind—but there it was, the blinking red light on his phone demanding attention. He tried to ignore it, but it flashed with such insistency he finally had to respond.

It was his secretary. The principal from Jenna's school had just called, and he needed to get there right away.

Not again! Please God, not again . . . the blinking light, the tone of voice; it was too familiar. He turned pale. Dreading what he might hear, he didn't ask for details. A year ago his wife Darlene had been on her way to that same school to pick Jenna up for a ninth grade soccer game. A truck blasted through a red light and T-boned her. Within moments firemen were working furiously with the Jaws-of-Life to get her broken body out of the car, but it was no use. She was lifeless as a china doll. The flashing red light and his secretary's tone were the same then as now...

He replaced the receiver, muttered a quick excuse to his three colleagues, and quickly walked out of his office. As he hurried by his secretary's desk, she gave him the same fearful and sympathetic look she had that time a year ago.

He took the same elevator down as he did then. The same ad for the same cafeteria was pasted on the same elevator walls; the same picture of the same food was still there.

A sob caught in his throat. He suppressed it.

The elevator . . . so damn slow—couldn't they at least change the picture?

He got in his Beamer in the garage, but his mind was already at the school. The car seemed to drive itself, turning left at the drugstore on the corner of Walnut and right at the gas station, four blocks down to the school, with no conscious input from him.

He had been taking Jenna to school over that same route for a year. Ever since the accident. Picking her up too, though not for soccer practice. Jenna had quit soccer. Quit everything—writing for the school paper, acting in the plays, cheerleading, even talking on the phone with her friends. Mostly she stayed in her room with the shades drawn and the door closed. And she didn't listen to music anymore. She used to be his sunshine girl, smiling only when she wasn't laughing.

But not anymore.

Oh God...

Darlene's face had been smashed. He had chosen a closed coffin. Jenna wanted him to open it so she could say good-bye to her mother, her best friend. He didn't want to do it, but he did. A mistake. Jenna hadn't been the same since.

She and Darlene had done everything together; shopped for brightly colored clothes, walked in the rain, danced to teeny bop tunes in the kitchen while cooking, baking or washing dishes. Everything was fun for them.

No more. Jenna didn't laugh any more. Her stylish preteen clothes hung unworn in the closet. She now chose brown, sometimes black. She rarely talked. It had been a year. He had waited for her to heal, but she only got worse. Now this.

He pulled into the parking lot at school and forced himself out of the car. A security guard offered to take him to the principal's office. Judging by the look on his face, the guard already knew what had happened.

Fearful and hesitant, he approached the principal's waiting rom. His chest was so tight he could hardly breathe. As he stood before the receptionist, he saw she too was apprehensive, as though sitting on tragic news she was not free to divulge.

She told him he was expected, that he should just knock and go in. He hesitated in front of the heavy door for a short moment. What horrible news was waiting for him behind this solid core door with imitation brass doorknob?

He took a deep breath, gingerly knocked, and opened the door.

He stopped, unable to release the doorknob for fear of collapsing. The walls and floor appeared gray, but he was dimly aware they might only seem that way because his vision was fading. The principal's desk was gray too, cold institutional steel, and there were no chairs for visitors.

A tinge of anger began replacing the despair. The anger grew as he realized he would be made to stand like an ordinary suppliant while his eminence fed him the details of this latest tragedy.

He tightened his hold on the knob.

The principal got up, came around the desk and adjusted his ridiculous tweed jacket with the leather patches at the elbow. Who did he think he was, an Oxford Don? A little man with a squeaky voice, he was saying something like . . . terrible thing . . . never had this happen before in my school . . . so much mess to clean up after her . . . can't have classes this afternoon . . . the students are out of control . . . no atmosphere for academic pursuits . . . was such a nice girl . . . a tragedy . . . and it's all her fault.

He was really angry now. All the little man cared about was his damn school and his spotless record. Solid core or not, he just might tear the doorknob out and plant it in the principal's skull.

By now the principal was pointing a trembling finger at something in the corner of the room hidden by the opened door. He was saying, "She started a food fight in the cafeteria."

He looked behind the door. There was Jenna, standing erect with her head held high and her arms folded on her chest. She had the light in her eyes that he loved but hadn't seen since Darlene's death, and she was grinning with defiance and delight. It had taken a year, but in the end, the spirit of his sunshine girl had burst back into life, and neither school authority nor the principal's anger could suppress it.

"Jenna!" he exclaimed, "Thank God! I thought . . ."

The principal continued his petulant sputtering, but neither father nor daughter paid the least attention. He stooped to embrace the girl. "never mind what I thought . . . oh Honey, I'm so proud of you!"

Tom Murphy

Tom Murphy is a People's Poetry Festival-Corpus Christi committee member. Murphy's books & CDs: American History (Slough Press, 2017), co-edited Stone Renga (Tail Feather, 2017), chapbook, Horizon to Horizon (Strike Syndicate, 2015), CDs "Live from Del Mar College" (BOW Productions, 2015), and "Slams from the Pit" (BOW Productions, 2014).

Obituary (muwashshaha)

In this God forsaken Bible
Rust Belt, Margaret Screws
Lived 98 years before going
To the Lord on November 19th
2016 at Mount Carmel CC.

    A dedicated nurse, who
        Learned her asses and lube trade
In the same hospital, she was born,
St. Paul's in Big D
As Margaret Ann Thurmon.

Moved to Kermit with her friend Janie
To nurse that West Texas big sky
At Robinson McClure Hospital
Where she gave a shot of penicillin
To her love, George Dewey "Pete" Screws.

    Humble Margaret screws
Pete's Fitz-Willie and pops
Out eight children before
Sun Oil Company shipped them
To San Isidro Sun Oil Field.

A school nurse, then a quick in 'n out.
The Kingsville Record's headline
"Margaret Screws Bishop
Now Screws in Premont."
Nurse of Brock County, humble, butt-proud.

Oh, Saint Teresa of the Infant Flower Catholic church of
      Premont!
How do we know Margaret Screws?
      The eight kids' 19 grandchildren
      Their 39 great grandchildren
      and their 3 great great grandchildren.

Her boys weren't all that proud or humble.
After childhood torment, teasing and torture
Two of the sons changed their name to Crews.
The five girls all married, thus taking their husbands' name.
Except for David Screws in Stephenville.

Remember, when you're pressing the button
While you're lying in that hospital bed,
mainlining meds and saline solution,
plus, filling up that colostomy bag,
remember, "Oh nurse?" Margaret Screws.

Richard Brautigan's Other Suicide

Why are we looking at the Golden Gate Bridge
from this perspective
as if we're on our way
down to the water

after having got
the guts to jump.
It is a nice foggy day
though. Foghorns play

an interesting melody in six,
no, seven tones; splat.

Then Again, On the Road
(two steps from losing it)

Not the happy go lucky fool
They pop up like tombstones
Beyond the lichgate
Straight from old English
The horrors of a life

After the last family generation
Convulsed on the floor after croaking
I love you
The shambles continue to exude like blood sweat
A mixture of Burke's two sublimes
Terror may be winning

There is an exit at the back of this room
It's just a quiet pop
Who knows what's on the other side
Though the stairs, if they're even there,
lead downward
Deepest circles of Alighieri inferno

I'll just sight see
If nobody minds too much
Just show me where you place
The colonel.

You Tender Hogs

You tender hogs
rip the world into shreds

speed the process of disintegration
challenge the good

in the petty
disgusting

simplicity of selfishness.
Tired and aching

in weakness
nearly impossible

to decipher
the geometry of your egotism—

everything is clotted
a disgusting network

in the last stages of fractures
still incomprehensible shape and form

perched on the edge—it falls
into nothingness rot

soft unprotected
membranes dying

bloody fingers
take your food

orange bells rung
broke your code

he said, "you remind me
of my 3rd husband."

she said, "you remind me
of my first cadaver

half in the bag
and cold to the touch."

Olivia Noble

Olivia Noble is a writer, painter, and Humanities major at Yale University, and an erstwhile resident of Corpus Christi. She attended King High School and took English classes from Joseph Wilson.

Making Friends

Play the moth game, inspired by the short stories of V. Woolf. The game goes like this: walk around from room to room until you have enough dead moths to fill each hand, which comes to about a cup and a quarter in a standard glass Pyrex. Another word for a double-handful is a yepsen. This group of moths you've picked up is now your first friend.

Draw with a pinched-out match tip on the white bottom of your sink. Turn the disposal into an unblinking all-seeing eye. This friend is good for staring contests and quick moralizing glances. It will look at you until its lids become runny. (The disposal should not be a new friend. It is loud and old and eats too much.)

Anything can be a friend if you try hard enough. Two faucets running in different rooms are now in conversation. Sometimes it's unwise to interrupt, but even on bad days you can always listen.

You can find them while you're drinking your maple milk at the window. On the streets all of your new car friends have snub-noses, like cats. The Volvo can be a little distant but at least it's direct.

Take off your shoes and arrange them in a clutter that you would never have left – oh, look, a friend must have kicked off their shoes in a hurry. It works, I promise.

Cut the bottoms off a few yellow pears and set them on their new stable bases. Look carefully for the bumps and brown marks that could be freckles, or even real dimples. Say, "I have missed seeing all your lovely faces!"

The moth collective is jealous now. Be on guard with your new friends. Their disapproval is a heavy thing.

One day you may wake up and find that the shirts on the clothesline are already such well-intentioned friends that you didn't even have to clip them up yourself. Their pale cuffs tumble and wave from the lawn. Pour the rest of your milk, which is now too warm, over the side of the porch and into the hostas. They might be taking things a little fast, but who are you to object?

Jose Olivares

Jose Olivares was born in Corpus Christi. He graduated from Roy Miller High School, and the University of Texas at Austin, Texas A&I University Kingsville, and Texas A&M University Corpus Christi. He worked as a secondary mathematics teacher, middle school principal and Corpus Christi Independent School District mathematics consultant and as adjunct professor of mathematics at Texas A&M CC. Jose and his wife Tomacita have three children who are also graduates of UT Austin. Their daughter Liana Gonzales is an attorney in Corpus Christi and daughter Mariela Olivares is also at attorney and law school professor at Howard University in Washington DC. Their son Jose Luis is a graphic computer artist in Portland, Oregon. They have four grandchildren.

Please Close the Windows

"Please close the windows, the air is burning my face" my younger sister cried as we drove to California seeking work as migrant workers. My parents had loaded the family (five children ages 17, 15, 13, 10, 4) into the car and headed cross country to the Bakersfield area. Two older siblings did not join us—one was married and the other was serving in the U.S. Army. I was 15.

Our car did not have air conditioning, but the desert air blowing into the car was so hot that we alternated closing and opening the windows. My Mother would constantly place a wet towel over my Father's head and shoulder in order to cool his body.

We worked picking grapes, peaches, potatoes and tomatoes. Our home was in one of the many labor camps in the area. Our shelter was a metal structure that felt like a furnace in the hot summer days. Our shelter had no electricity, running water or bathroom facilities. Group facilities were available for our use.

Children worked alongside their families and contributed in the daily pickings. We generally worked eight to ten hours each day.

My brother taught me to drive a car that summer. It was a Chevy with a standard shift. One of my greatest pleasures that summer was driving to a corner store on Fridays and drinking a quart of chocolate milk without having to share with my siblings. "When I grow up, I will buy all the chocolate milk I want," I would tell my brother.

That was the summer of 1962. César Chávez and the United Farmworkers Union that sought to improve working and living conditions for migrant workers would come years later.

Levántate Mi Hijo
by
Jose Olivares

--José, levántate mi hijo, ya son las seis-- my Mother said as she woke me up. I waited for her to leave and then started crying silently. I was about 12 years old.

My nightly dreams included episodes of picking cotton. I picked cotton during the day and then I picked cotton during my sleep. I remember being exhausted in the mornings, but I gave myself the privilege of crying only once. I did not tell anyone. I felt I could not take a day off.

We generally worked ten to twelve hours a day in the cotton fields of South Texas. I always felt it was my job to pick cotton, as much as I could, every day. Most of our family worked in the cotton fields during the summers.

Each week my parents would give me about one dollar to spend and our earnings were used to provide for our family. I could count on a new shirt, pants, and sometimes shoes for the start of the new school year. I worked in the cotton fields from grade school through my sophomore year in high school.

Joel Jay Ortiz

Joel Jay Ortiz has been reading, writing, and performing poetry since 1991. He started at various open mikes, reading poetry with musicians, and then continued when open mike with spoken word began appearing. He has been published in various indie zines and been the guest poet at readings in Austin and Corpus Christi. He also hosted open mikes throughout the years. His poetry tends to be literary with literary allusions and pentameters that agree with music, due to his love of music and ability to play guitar and piano. He wishes the world read more poetry and loves to hear poets express themselves, especially in a venue where poets can be themselves.

sometimes you're just damned

sometimes you're just damned
books, that spine I love, curving at the right
pages. Her dog ears I flip in my mind, kissing
each sentence I injest into my system.
I've given it all up so I can enjoy a few
paragraphs of intelligent chatter
I've ignored many possibilites many lives so I could
stick to those dirty words
i've taken ferries to countless libraries
and devoured each lover from its brain and secluded
many covers i just blew away
in my own i have stolen unmade masterpieces
and gave my full attention to such minds games the best
of the race have created
to be seated in rooms of your brain, you move so subtly

from

    reading to writing. what you read becomes the very word

you

    write. These fictions, these tigres de los suenos, as that
educated prick so rightfully wrote

life is very much like a book
you can either take your time and inject the wisdom
or enjoy it fast & move on to other works of pulp
in the end it comes from someone's library, it was somebody's book
it was my book but now i see that the mending department doesn't
even want to put together my torn book
i'll just let it fly off in all directions, my pages fly away like icarus, with no
destination
destination can be substituted for destruction
a reconsctruction of tales with no heads
for we dread what poetry can give birth to
oh poetry, i'd die for you
anytime, anyplace
POETRY!-----OPEN YOUR EARS FOR WE'VE GOT TO RECITE THE TIMES
POETRY!-----KEEPS US TIGHT AS SHRUNKEN SWEATERS
POETRY!-----HOW I WANT NOTHING ELSE BUT POETRY.

Zoe Elise Ramos

Zoe Elise Ramos was born and raised in Corpus Christi. She studies chemistry and creative writing at Texas A&M-CC. She has been a poetry editor for the Windward Review since 2016. Her work has been featured in the Switchgrass Review, Sink Hollow, and the Sagebrush Review. She was also awarded a 1st place prize in the 2018 Scissortail undergraduate creative writing contest. Her latest work (in progress) is a multimedia zine which pays homage to social media culture and its impact on communication styles.

two lost children and a pile of sticks to make something of

"Dear, your buds are all there is to breathe and the gift of heaven's scent's polonium in the well. When sprouts first burst through winds, all leaves are cleaned of graffitied need, gaudy paint of desire's biting, buzzing alive like uncaught gems. They are all breathed as the shoots force our petals into the wild breezes above—oversized garden with no keeper. And us, paled and verdant shrubberies are grasses struck envious of flowers, vivid fictile freedom's sight, vibrant of glass vindication's color, potent ubiquity's house unheeded over these broke shoulders. And we fill up on stolen peace all just to loosen limbs. So kiss me, kiss me here"

tangled roots

We are under the trellis of Nueva Vita, a garden that murmurs with heaves of impatiens. From somewhere, the scream of autos tears at the plum of gingersnaps. They coil and fold their leaves into boats. I hold your hand while leaning, watching passerines blowing kisses to one another. This is just as you like though we are not *llamas gemelas*; we are the stems of an allium shooting off in diverging directions, never to touch but always close, borne from the same fruits. We swell from the heat of that glowing suspension and the sun is singing. It singes your skin into milky champurrado. Liberated winds hold their shining ends as if a vessel. And hummingbirds bait and stick us as we turn to sap all over the tree scenery. An SUV bares its teeth across the way to remind us that we are machinery. You cup your hands into buds and hold them over these ears. Your words are soil to me with my ligaments of buzzing bees and veins rippling with honey. "*Suelo bueno, tomar este corazón y comerlo.*" The cherub fountains of flushed marble cry themselves onto the floor. Brown translucence melts into creases between planets, with our shoes dripping into softness, wasted pollen stolen on fingertips. Now, we no longer stand but float atop the white and scarred swing, still creaking back and forth like the hands on a clock. *Usted toma estas flores picante como el suyo en su boca.* I give you my roots and you give me your flowers.

Esther Bonilla Read

Esther Bonilla Read was born and raised in Calvert, Texas, a small town in Central Texas. She graduated from Baylor University and began teaching school in Corpus Christi, Texas. This became home for her and her husband Nolan K. Read and their four children. She writes on a variety of subjects: her family; school; and of various incidents that have occurred in her life. She has been published by various newspapers; Chicken Soup for the Latino Soul and several anthologies and magazines.

The Lesson

It was right before Christmas, and we fifth graders in Mrs. Pietsch's classroom were an excited group of chattering students. WWII was over. It was now peace time, and it was a time to be happy.

Most students in our school didn't have an abundance of material things, but we didn't know that. And the students who had the least were the children of itinerant or sharecropping farm workers. Some came to school barefooted. Others wore the same clothes over and over. No matter how much starch the mother used before she ironed the girls' dresses, they were the same ones worn week after week.

Suddenly midst the chatter we heard our teacher Mrs. Pietsch raise her voice. She told us to be quiet as she had an announcement. She asked, "Who took a five dollar bill out of my purse?"

Everyone was quiet. We looked at one another with questioning faces. Only the voice of two students walking down the hallway could be heard. Some students in our class whispered to one another. Two or three chairs scraped the floor. Then one boy laughingly said, "Ben took it." I knew my brother Ben didn't take anything from anyone. He never would.

Mrs. Pietsch recognized it as a joke. Nonetheless, she responded, "He didn't take anything. His father used to work with my husband, and he is an honest man." That put that suggestion/joke to rest.

Again quietness. Mrs. Pietsch continued with her Civics lesson. Still, I couldn't get it out of my mind. A five dollar bill; I had never even held one in my life, and I think very few students, if any, in my class had experienced that either.

Mrs. Pietsch didn't mention it again. Eventually, a friend told me which classmate had taken it. She left school during our lunch hour and walked to town with the money to buy her little siblings toys at Kress, our local Five and Ten Cent Store. It seems because it was winter the farmers had little work for their sharecroppers and money was hard to come by. The girl hated the thought that the little ones in her family would wake up and have nothing on Christmas Day. Thus, she had taken the money so the little ones would have toys. She wasn't thinking of herself, but of them.

Although I wondered how the problem would be settled, we followed the teacher's lead and never mentioned the loss. Through that incident I learned much from Mrs. Pietsch. You can be strict but compassionate. There comes a time when diplomacy and gracefulness are to be used, and this was one of those times.

It could be that the student might have brought the teacher a dollar a month or something like that to pay her back. However the issue was resolved, we continued at school as though nothing had happened. But I can't help but think back to Mrs. Pietsch.

Yes, Mrs. Pietsch taught us a great deal, and the lessons did not always come out of textbooks.

Mona Schroeder

Mona Schroeder is a writer and former librarian who lives in Corpus Christi, Texas. This excerpt is from a novel called Random Acts about Cecilia Kendall, a woman struggling to put her life back together after a great loss. Determined never to be hurt again, her solution is to shut out the world until a chance encounter forces her to reconsider her choices and to wonder if one random act might begin to be healed by another.

Random Acts
(Novel excerpt)

Cecilia Kendall watched the mid-morning El Paso sun slip through the closed blinds in her breakfast room. It was determined, always trying to sneak in where it wasn't wanted. She poured herself another cup of coffee—black. She took it that way now – strong, black Colombian coffee, unpolluted by milk or cream or sugar or by international cream substitutes that were supposed to spice up one's life by drinking them.

She sat at the table and thumbed through the mail without interest. Richard had brought it in for her one last time before packing his bags and leaving. She supposed she would have to retrieve it from the mailbox herself from now on which would mean changing out of her bathrobe, something she was reluctant to do. She wondered if she could persuade the mailman to shove it through a slot in the door if she had one put in. Or would she have to put in a whole new door?

Cecilia made a mental note and resolved to check into it later. Groceries, too. She could have them delivered – not that she needed many. Coffee and some frozen dinners perhaps. There was a certain morose appeal to the thought of her self-imposed solitary confinement – at the idea of mail being silently thrust through the door, of hermetically sealed frozen dinners forced through the mail slot one at a time. The coffee might present a problem, but that could be worked out, she was sure. Maybe Juan Valdez could schlep it over on that donkey of his.

Schlep. Where had that word come from, she wondered? She wasn't Jewish, wasn't anything really. She hadn't been to church in years. "Schlep," she repeated aloud, rolling it off her tongue slowly. It was not a word she would normally use, but today was not a normal day, not the morning after her husband of seventeen years had left her.

Yet the knowledge that Richard would not be coming home to her today or perhaps ever again did not move her, not in the way she would have thought a year ago. A year ago everything in her life had changed with one single act. Another drive-by shooting. Only this time the victim hadn't been a stranger who died. This time a gun had claimed the life of someone she loved, her fifteen-year-old son Josh.

It should be a law of the universe that no parents be forced to survive their children, Cecilia thought. Without Josh, she felt as if a part of her were missing – the best part. What was she now? She wasn't a mother, no longer a wife either. She had quit her job, her friends, and her husband had quit her. She had no close living relatives. She wasn't someone's daughter or sister or aunt or niece. What did that make her? She was 37 years old and had no label, an unsettling thought.

Cecilia reflected on all the ways she had tried to fill the hole that Josh's absence had left in her life. Alcohol. Xanax. Valium. Even, unbelievably for her, an affair. Although "affair" was a rather grandiose term for the experience. Would 30 minutes in a cheap motel count as an affair? Nothing had transpired that night worth a scarlet letter. She'd had more interest in the brightly wrapped condoms the man had produced – and certainly more contact. Latex lust in the 21st century. Safe sex. Was sex ever really safe? Was any contact with another human being completely safe?

She hadn't thought of the affair as an act of betrayal or even of revenge, more as an unsatisfactory attempt to hold the memories and the awful emptiness at bay for a few moments. An act of survival. The knowledge that Richard had been having an affair for some time had not failed to penetrate her otherwise dulled consciousness, but it hadn't been a motivating factor for her. Cecilia couldn't blame Richard, not really. Their own love-making had become almost nonexistent in the past year, and so when she had detected all the signs of an unfaithful husband – traces of lipstick, a hint of unfamiliar perfume on his shirts, his socks worn inside out as if hastily put back on – she hadn't been shocked. Disappointed maybe, in a philosophical way. But was it disappointment in Richard or the fact that he didn't bother to hide his indiscretions any better than he had? She could accept infidelity but not carelessness?

After Richard left, Cecilia hadn't cried or asked "Why me?" She knew that long before he left her, she had left him. She hadn't made it a physical separation, but it had been there nonetheless. As the door closed behind Richard, she had felt sadness, tinged with a certain relief. She felt free, but from what she wasn't exactly sure – free from obligations perhaps, from unspoken demands, free from the guilt she felt every time she looked at him, wishing that she could love him again but knowing that she couldn't.

Richard would probably ask her for a divorce soon. One thing generally followed another like that, like a child's game of dominoes careening wildly across the floor. Impossible to stop once started. Cecilia wasn't afraid of divorce, but she didn't like the sound of it, the finality of it. The "ever after" without the "lived happily" part in front. Now it was simply "lived."

Looking down, Cecilia realized that she had sorted the mail by habit – bills in one pile, personal letters or cards in another, and junk mail set aside for recycling. She shuffled through the bill pile again – gas, electric, two phone bills. Two? She examined them more closely. One was hers, but the other was to a Meryl Stephenson at 224 Flynn, instead of 244. The mailman had made a mistake. Wondering if there were more, she thumbed through the mail again. Sure enough, more envelopes addressed to Ms. Meryl Stephenson or Charles Stephenson, same address – a card, an application for a credit card, and an envelope from a doctor's office. She wondered how long she had been getting this Meryl person's mail. Should she return it? Would Meryl or Charles be worried, waiting for their phone bill, wondering what could have happened to it?

Cecilia sighed. She supposed she would have to return it. It would mean changing from her bathrobe into street clothes, putting on shoes, running a comb through her hair, but she would have to do it. All that trouble because of a simple mistake. A nagging sense of decorum forbade her from taking the mail down the street in her bathrobe and slippers. It would give new meaning to the word "schlep."

John Swinburn

John Swinburn called Corpus Christi home from the time he was five years old until he graduated from Richard King High School in 1972. Corpus Christ was where he developed a framework for understanding the world. He earned his Bachelor of Art's degree from the University of Texas at Austin, and eventually formed an association management company with his wife. Since his retirement, Swinburn has used his time to write, relax, and restructure his world view and perspective on life, a work in progress. He and Janine live in the Ouachitas in central Arkansas. Swinburn posts regularly on his blog at www.johnswinburn.com. "It's not for the faint of heart," he says of his blog. "One day I may use it as a journal, the next as a repository for my fiction or poetry, and the next an outlet for an odd mixture of left-leaning and libertarian political rants."

On Open Water

Early that morning, at daybreak, a shallow, nearly opaque layer of water-hugging mist flowed in through the quiet marina. Faith watched it roll in, a slow-motion wave of dense wax sliding in from the open water. It was an odd fog bank, low and creamy, just a few feet above the surface. The masts and decks of boats in the marina were visible, but everything below deck remained hidden. That impenetrable layer of light grey concealed the boardwalk, too, leaving only an orderly cluster of boats rising from a dull, fictile grey cloud.

No one would be foolish enough to venture out in that fog, Faith reasoned, so she thought she could safely assume hers would be the only boat on the open water. She could see the lights of only one other boat. She slogged through the knee-high cloud along the wooden planks between the slips, blind to the boardwalk, so she judged her position by staying equidistant from the boats on either side, safely away from the dock's edge.

On a clear day, the loud chatter of seagulls would have broken the stillness of the early morning air. Small flocks of pelicans would have glided a few feet above the surface of the water in search of breakfast. The air would have been heavy with the scent of salt water and seaweed. But on this foggy morning, the birds were waiting for better visibility. Silence enshrouded the boats and the marina and beyond, where open water slept beneath a heavy veil. The sweet aromas of salt and fish filled Faith's nostrils, though the fog muted those scents of the sea.

Until she had moved to the island a decade earlier, Faith had never set foot on a sailboat. In ten years' time, though, she had become an accomplished sailor, learning much of what she knew by watching other people sail, reading, and watching YouTube videos. Repetition of the sailor's art, too, contributed to her skills and built her into a strong and powerful mariner. Open water represented liberty to Faith, freedom from the stifling regimens she associated with life back on the U.S. mainland, the boredom she had so loathed that she had abandoned it, at age forty-six, for the island life.

Her boat's slip was at the far end of the marina, the very last one on the northwest side.

As she climbed aboard Norteña, her 28-foot Catalina, she heard a voice. "Miss! Miss! You goin' out now? Too much fog, Miss! Better wait."

She couldn't see him, but she recognized the voice as Lucius Labade, the de facto manager of the marina who possessed neither the official title nor salary that would normally accompany the role.

"Hi, Lucius! Nobody else is going to be out in this fog. I'll be careful!"

"Oh, Miss, you never know 'bout that water. Better safe, Miss. Better safe. I think you wait until fog lifts, okay?" His voice was closer now, but she still couldn't see him.

"I appreciate your concern, Lucius, I really do. But I'll be fine. Don't you worry."

Suddenly, the little man appeared in front of her, his face directly in front of and level with her breasts.

"Miss, please listen; wait just awhile, okay?"

His hot breath, which she felt through the mesh fabric of her bikini top, startled her. He was just inches away, close enough that he had to raise his eyes and tilt his head to see her face.

"Lucius, you know I'm not going to wait, don't you? I promise, I'll be fine."

"Oh, Miss, I know you one hard-headed woman. I wish you listen to Lucius this time. This fog not like normal. This too thick."

"You're a sweet old man, Lucius. I love you for worrying about me! I'm going to be just fine. I'll see you in a few hours."

Lucius, at sixty-four, was not much older than Faith. Sixty-four years of salt water and sun had stolen the youth from his skin, replacing it with ragged ancient leather and black dots, lesions of unknown but apparently benign origin.

Faith stood in stark contrast to the island native. Her toned body commanded hungry stares from men. Their undisguised lust was the only truly unpleasant aspect of island life. Though rarely did any of them continue making overtures once rebuffed, they did not hide their lechery. That open display reminded Faith of her ex-husband's unrestrained carnal desire—for her in the early years of their marriage and for anyone else younger and firmer in its waning years.

Lucius acknowledged defeat. "Okay, Miss, but promise be careful. And when you back you tell me, okay?"

"Yes, Lucius, I'll let you know when I get back. I've got my radio with me, too, so if I need help, you'll hear me calling."

Faith untied Norteña, coaxed the diesel motor to life, and maneuvered her out of the slip toward open water. Until she could catch a breath of wind, the diesel would be the Catalina's only power.

***

Lucius stood, his eyes fixed on her boat, as Norteña slid almost silently away from the marina, the diesel barely growling as it thrust the boat forward. He continued watching until the vessel became a speck in the distance. As he turned his gaze away from the disappearing boat, Lucius noticed another craft slowly move out from the far end of the marina, the only other slip with a light. He squinted to see which boat it was, but it was too far away. He walked in the direction of the slip from which the boat had come. Finally, he determined that the light belonged to the empty slip for Abrázame, a boat owned by a relative newcomer to the island, Drake Pool.

Lucius had overheard Pool making a pass at Faith. Pool, who was in his sixties, thought of himself as a lady's man. During the two months he had been on the island, he had been involved in several unfortunate incidents in which his "dates" had abruptly left his company after, according to their reports, Drake had groped them. Faith had been one of the women Pool attempted to seduce. Lucius remembered what happened.

"I have no interest in, nor patience for, men like you," she had said to Pool after he suggested, during a party at the island mayor's home, that they retire to an empty bedroom. Unwilling to accept her response at face value, Pool continued his pursuit.

"Listen, honey, you know and I know there's a shortage of men like me on this island and you already know I find you attractive. Do us both a favor and dispense with the obligatory objections because, you know, I don't take no for an answer."

Faith's eyes flashed and a brilliant red fireball ignited her cheeks. "Your conceit is astonishing, especially in light of the fact that neither your intellect nor your looks are doing you any favors. I am absolutely delighted there are no other men like you on this island, because we islanders loathe dealing with trash! Now, you will take no for an answer, Mr. Pool, and if I must give you that answer again, you will regret moving to this island! Do I make myself clear?"

Pool smirked. "Oh, yes ma'am. I know exactly what you're saying. Enjoy the rest of the parry, uh, I mean party."

Lucius hadn't heard the entire exchange, but he had been at the party and heard enough of the words and the way they were exchanged to know of Faith's displeasure with Pool. Lucius hadn't liked Pool from the moment he met the man. Pool had always been mean to Lucius, talking down to him, belittling him. Lucius glanced back at the slip where Faith's boat had been, then turned again toward Pool's empty slip.

"Best see about this," he muttered, his brow furrowing. He looked toward the slip that held his own boat. At first, his movements were measured and slow, but as he continued along the boardwalk, he picked up speed. By the time he reached the section of the docks where his boat was moored, his pace was as close to a run as his old body could do.

"Dammit, this not good, I just know is not good!" he said aloud. He unwound the ropes from the cleats on the port and starboard sides of his boat, both stern and bow, then pushed away from the dock with a long pole. His little boat, half the size of

Faith's, drifted a few feet into the pea soup fog; he started his electric trolling motor and steered the craft around the protective jetty and into open water, following the disrupted fog bank like a river.

Twenty minutes later, Lucius began to see signs that the fog was lifting, or perhaps simply melting into the surf. The morning sun was high enough to burn off the top of the bank. A light breeze, the sun's gift every morning when air began to warm, blew away the remnants of the fog is short order.

Though he welcomed the breeze, Lucius wasn't happy that the disrupted fog, which had left a bread-crumb trail to follow Pool, evaporated. The only way to follow him would be by sight. He pulled a pair of binoculars from a tray beneath the wheel and scanned the horizon in front of him. Initially, he could see nothing but sky and water, but after another scan he saw something that looked the size of a gnat, a mile or two in front of him. He steadied the binoculars against a wooden brace and looked intently at the gnat.

"Both of 'em; they both way in front of me."

Lucius hoisted a single sail and set out in the direction of the gnats on the horizon as fast as the sluggish breeze would take him. Though he knew it probably wouldn't help, he kept the trolling motor going full blast, as well.

He was surprised that he caught up to the two boats as quickly as he did; in less than forty-five minutes, he was within shouting distance of both vessels, neither of which was under sail. As he neared the two boats, he saw Pool drop anchor. From Norteña, Faith, whose boat was already at anchor, also watched Pool.

When Lucius was just a few hundred feet from the two boats, Pool turned toward him and scowled at his approach.

"Hey, Lucie, what are you doing out here?"

Faith turned in Lucius' direction, a quizzical look on her face.

"I came to make sure everybody okay; fog bank really bad and could come back. You go back in now, yes?"

"Lucius, don't you worry about us, we'll be fine. Mr. Pool seems to want to spend a little time out on the open water with me." Faith's smile suggested to Lucius that she was, indeed, fine.

Pool glared at Lucius. "Yeah, Lucie, you don't need to worry. Go on back to the island. We'll be fine. We just need a little privacy out here, you know?"

Lucius looked at Pool's smirk, then at Faith. "You sure? Miss, better if you go back now, okay?"

Pool's face turned red. "Listen, goddamn it! Get the hell out of here, Lucie! Got it? We want some privacy!"

Lucius looked at Faith again, a deep wrinkle in his brow and his head cocked in disbelief.

"Miss? You sure?"

"Lucius, you're a sweetheart, but I'll be fine! I really appreciate you coming all this way, but I'm just fine. I just want a little time with Mr. Pool, away from the prying eyes of the islanders, okay? And, please, let's keep this between us, all right? No need to start the gossip mill."

Pool sneered at Lucius. "Go on, Lucie! You heard the lady!"

Lucius started to open his mouth, but clinched his jaw, instead, and began to maneuver his boat away from the two at anchor. As he departed, he shouted back to Faith: "Miss, you tell me when you back, okay?"

"I will, sweetheart! Don't worry."

Lucius looked back again. When he saw Faith in the water, swimming toward Pool's boat, he grimaced. Tears filled his eyes and rolled down his cheeks.

Three hours later, when he saw Norteña come around the jetty, Lucius hurried toward Faith's boat slip. He waited as she approached the dock, waving at her as she coaxed the boat into the slip.

"I so glad you back, Miss!" he shouted. "I was afraid for you out there with Mr. Pool. You okay?"

"Of course, I'm fine, Lucius. You're so precious to have worried."

"I don't see Mr. Pool boat; he on his way back?"

"Lucius, I asked you if we could keep this to ourselves, right? Can we keep it to ourselves that you saw Pool out there?"

"Yes, Miss, sure. But where is he?"

"You never know what to expect out on open water, especially when you can't see what's right in front of you. Lucius, I learned my lesson. I won't do that again." She paused and said, "He won't either."

Lucius was confused for a moment, but then he began to understand, and the edges of his mouth turned up. She nodded, almost imperceptibly and returned the smile.

"Thank you, Lucius, for looking after me. I'm sorry I sent you away, but I needed to deal with Pool."

"You my good friend, Miss. Always look after you."

"And I truly appreciate that, Lucius. Yes, you are my good friend."

"Mr. Pool not gonna bother you no more."

"No, Lucius, I don't think he will," Faith said, and wrapped her right arm around his shoulders with a squeeze.

Neesy Tompkins

Neesy Tompkins was born in San Antonio but left for Port Aransas as soon as she graduated from High School. She and her then-husband ran a shrimp boat for several years. Later, she was employed in the restaurant and bar industries where she met many colorful characters that are reflected in the stories she writes. It wasn't until attending college, which was possible because of a Hurricane, that she was acknowledged as a writer by her winning of a National Essay Contest with her story entitled "The Gift." She graduated with a degree in Mass Communications and a Minor in History in May 2017, which is utilized in her current self-employment as a social media manager and advertising agency for local Port Aransas businesses. Along with writing, photography of the Island she adores is a passion.

The Life of a Ship

It was like any other day, the day my father died. Oblivious to the crying and runny noses on the other end of the phone line, it seemed surreal, like the way talking sounds through the fog across a ship channel, muffled. With shaky voices, they talked of arrangements.

Voices repeated that he was really gone, as I tried to comprehend how I was supposed to act. And this huge sense of nothingness overcame me, like trying to stay adrift through a dark sea of bitterness and disappointment, blindly searching for an answer that is not there as I attempted to feel what they were feeling.

After the funeral, after the law books and business had been divided and before returning to the Island, my share of possessions resulted in a cardboard box filled with ships that my father had collected throughout his years, always on his credenza shelves in his law office collecting dust. Some metal, others bamboo, and even an oil painting in cobalt blues of a Spanish galleon tossed upon stormy seas.

The box went into the storage room of my old mobile home, in the place I stored things that I didn't care to see. A junk room, cluttered with bird feathers and seashells, a rusty ironing board and old photographs of a life long ago known that had somehow changed so drastically to have tossed me here on this Island known as home for so long.

Home, such a strange word. How to define home? I was not born here but knew I belonged here. Here with the harsh Winters and a chill that reaches down the corridors of your heart, yet the ocean gave me comfort, like a warm blanket and a buffer between the world and me.

Until that day in August and a storm that drove in unsuspected, so only a few pair of clothing changes were taken as I loaded up for higher ground.

A week passed, holding my breath, stuck in a city with concrete and buildings that obliterated any chance of viewing a sunset. With an aching heart I returned, knowing that what was left might not be much after seeing video after video of first responders on social media, some of them close to my street but never my street exactly. Prepared for the worst, my feet trampled heavily through still wet and muddy ground, and a stench that was almost as unbearable as the mosquitos dive-bombed any flesh left uncovered.

My old mobile, what was left of it, lay on its side, white walls fallen like broken wings in the mud, weighted down by sewage and stinky mud. Everything was covered in a putrid brown color, the stench of rotting fish and seaweed halfway up the sides with wires exposed. Ironically, the kitchen shelves and dishes in the cupboards stood untouched, coffee mugs ready for a new morning and a new day. Searching through remnants for anything that might be salvaged, a few dead birds lay in awkward positions pointed the way on the saturated ground to where a book lay open. It was the only book found, Sue Monk Kidd's The Invention of Wings, pages still damp, barely legible and opened to expose a line reading "Let not your heart be troubled. Neither let it be afraid". And I started to cry. One of those long moaning cries that comes with the pain of letting go, and giving in.

It is odd the things that come to mind when you are searching through an invisible list, panicked at not recalling all the things stored that don't float to the top like cream; the ashes to my old cat that had just passed a few months earlier, a tiny box of my daughter's baby teeth, the bin of my grandmother's crocheted tablecloth.

As I raced trying to recall what else I was searching for, it was with panic that the ships came to mind. The box of my father's ships. Why did it matter? It mattered because that was all I ever had of my father. His dusty old ships that lay placid on a dormant wooden credenza in his office where the only light they ever saw was from fluorescent bulbs. Perhaps he collected them as his secret wishes of someday sailing the world from the bow of a schooner, free as the wind. And perhaps he knew that under my care, somehow those dusty ships were one step closer to the Ocean where they belonged. Yet, on that day when the wind came from the South, hot and humid, and the sweat dripping from my brow, the stench of death perforating through my clothes in the rising heat, I could not find his ships.

Looking back on that day now, it seems the Hurricane stirred up many things left hiding under the surface. Although nature can sometimes be relentless and cruel, she is always honest. And like the churning waters of a hurricane displacing things no longer useful, the ships under my care and possession had been tossed back into the Ocean and away from me. Perhaps it was my time to let go of things. His ashes, he wanted them scattered in the sea. Maybe someday that will be honored.

Months later, things are looking better. I have returned to the place where my family dwells, where his ashes sit on top of a mantle, collecting dust and far from any body of water. I too am far from the Sea because for now, that is where the currents have taken me. At times when I visit my old place by the Ocean, I still look for a sign of a toy mast, a tattered sail somewhere lodged on a tree limb that I somehow overlooked. Still nothing.

I like to think that somewhere on the horizon a few small toy ships bob on an Ocean of mirrored glass, sailing off into the sunset, because that's what ships do best. I like to think that people are like ships, passing one another if meant to, never knowing where the tides and currents will take you. And perhaps someday, I will catch a glimpse of one of those ships that used to sit on my father's credenza, doing now what ships do best, sailing free. That, I like to think, is the reason my father entrusted me to inherit his beloved ships, perhaps because he knew they would be one step closer to the Ocean that he so admired.

For my father, I pray he has found peace, perhaps riding on the high seas of a Spanish Galleon of a cobalt blue Ocean, free like the ships he used to collect. And as for me, I am no longer afraid of letting go. That is the lesson this Hurricane brought me, no fear.

Ana Varela

By the time you're reading this, I hope to know more than I did when I sat down to tell you about myself. As it stands, I graduated from California State University of Long Beach with degrees in International Studies and Chinese Studies. I moved to Corpus Christi and help run a business repairing vintage motorcycles. I spend my free time placing international students with volunteer host families. I also coordinate a local group, the Culture Exchange of Corpus Christi which promotes cultural connections and inspired conversations about community. I write regularly for myself and most recently I enjoy collaborating locally. I welcome change.

My Desert Jay and I

The valley knew that it would change my life forever. The longer that I spent in it, the more sure I was of where I needed to be. Nothing could be the same after that summer in the desert.

I met Jay in the three days that I spent at the end of spring in the Joshua Tree dessert. I would not leave for good until the come and go of a year of seasons. If I was once a seed I had grown into a mesquite, and I was finally enjoying my shade. Before, I had wandered content, well-nourished from the freedom of decisions that had led me to this event. When I reached the desert, I gave in to a restful time and listened, for once, to the message of a music festival. If "music is the soul of life" then the desert is the body from which energy might manifest as humming, the vibrations as song. I met my Jay in Joshua Tree, and, one day, I flew away with him.

My first winter with Jay was a high-desert January and a world of wonder. I drove the three hours from Los Angeles, as I had done so many times throughout the summer, to reach our paradise in the desert. The last hour of the drive, heading up the mountain after a windmill valley, was hard on the car but easy on the mind. I passed the small but popular Joshua Tree city, catering to the tourists that came from around the world to visit the national park, the businesses boutique with faux-desert facades. Farther up the road Twentynine Palms -- an even smaller bucolic town that most only know if they have heard of the military base. Two different cities, like two very different beasts, feeding on that which keeps them growing. Turning off the main street there, I drove for a quarter of an hour more as the asphalt turned into dirt road. Not too far in the distance, with its red stripe around its side, the 1970's El Rey camper was my minds favorite sight. I imagined that I could hear Jay's small dog panting as he listened for my tires driving up the property. I was moments from Jay's smile and feeling the weight of the wine glass in my hand.

The sky in winter matched Jay's eyes -- a crisp and clean bright, blue grey. By morning, I was happy to be in the El Rey, warmed by the closeness of our bodies. If this had been August, the camper would be empty by midday, and we would be somewhere else searching for shade. Winter called for a noontime wandering. When the morning freeze had melted under the sun, we set out from our cozy home. Imitating the flower buds of the cacti around us, we wrapped up in layered bundles, bursting with anticipation for spring. Vast and limitless, ours was the most beautiful backyard in the world. Except for the few trails we had worn around the property, we explored in a new direction every day. There was every shape of twisting branch discovered for each pairless shoe found. When the afternoon warmed enough, we stopped anywhere in a greasewood bush field to drink wine, laugh, and watch as the stars appeared.

The Joshua Tree seemed the greatest teacher, the desert the greatest classroom. For it to survive, the Joshua Tree gave parts of itself to the desert; fruit for the sloth (extinct to humans) and seeds for Yucca Moth larvae to eat. When the flowers bloom in spring, the appreciative moth pollinates other trees. It is a thousand year old dance of coevolution. The philosophy of the Joshua Tree was simple; keep only that which you need to survive and a partner to help you grow- the rest is too heavy to carry.

Jay had a bird's eye view of the world, and could see farther than I ever could alone. He could see where the wind would blow, dropping pieces of desert trash and treasures in a secret sand bowl. It was a long valley, hidden between a row of small mountains and sand dunes. Burnouts and storms and time had turned parts into pieces and sections to shreds. Collecting our favorite fragments of broken plates, plastics, and metals, Jay and I spent afternoons creating our mosaics. Longing for a body of water, the sound of a crashing wave, or the salt saturated spray of ocean mist, he brought a sea creature to life in the dry desert. With teeth of glass and shotgun shells for scales a devilish angler fish appeared from the sand. Once, a friend, stopping in our desert on a roadtrip across the country, painted a monarch over a wide boulder in our secret mosaic sand bowl. Before him, that boulder had looked like an abandoned Volkswagen bug in the distance. Then, it was as if the butterfly had flown swiftly into the side of the boulder and left her color splattered all over the sand. So vast, in fact, was this mosaic valley, that when we returned to find the massive monarch, with a wingspan twice as large as mine, she seemed to have flown off. Perhaps the Volkswagen had suddenly driven away.

Nothing dies in the desert. A seemingly dry greasewood, when its bare branch snaps, reveals a jade green center, ready to feed the new leaves of spring. If something begins to lose life, it crumbles over the sands' surface and smooths to preservation becoming an important particle of the ever growing land. Everything becomes the desert again.

The first time I crashed a motorcycle I fell into the soft embrace of the desert. The deep trail behind me snaked its way more sharply the closer to where I lay. Jay hadn't seen me yet. I didn't want him to think that I was hurt. I unburied myself from the sand and, despite the pain in my shin, walked over to the other side of the little red Honda to pull it up. By the time Jay had noticed, I was loading onto the bike again. I only fell once more that day as we were leaving the mosaic valley, burying my front tire into the side of one of the dunes. Again the snickering snake led to exactly the point where I was splayed across the sand.

Summer had gone months before but the grab of its rays still burned like yesterday in our memories. Each blazing day of that season, when the rocks and the trees and the mountains began to see their shadows, we set off on another ride. The buzzing motorbikes echoed through the canyons we explored. The world hummed to the tune of our adventures. Eager for curious visitors and luring us in with their shade, we rode up to the mouth of the hungry caves. Abandoned mines that had no notion of time. It would be weeks before the next desert riders would find them again. Leaving behind the cold and burning superheated summer surface world to the lizards, we walked into the earth and entered the cool, endless darkness. Deep blue turquoise streaks lined the inside of the otherwise rough earth; perfect lines of oxidized copper led us deeper and deeper inside.

Like Plato's allegory of the cave, I wondered if my high-desert stories made sense to many city dwellers or the strictly social media savants. Would they see the value in the voids or the expanses of the desert? How might I convey the worth in the woe of an abandoned mine? After allowing our internal temperatures to drop, and our inner thoughts to cool and calm, we wander back to see how the sand of the summer had changed. Time is measured by the sun, and it waits for no one.

We were never lost following the cooing and whispering hints of the wind, then the allure of the light. Emerging from the mine, we were enveloped in a warm embrace by the two; the sky and the sun welcomed us again. Unlike a city, where the alleys at night should be avoided, this world would not punish me for walking into the darkness.

Regardless of the season, each morning my eyes were opened by the gentle kiss of sunrise, calling for me to come outside to face the rising Ra. These 2,700 feet above sea level are pure -- similar to starving the muscles for oxygen, so does the elevation strengthen the soul. There is little room for the toxic smog of my mind that I bring with me from the city each drive and soon it is all taken away by the very same wind the urges me forward. I must have followed that very wind to that Spring festival that took me away with Jay forever. Each day in the desert since then, we did as the animals did and looked to find shade at noon otherwise, we would be bake in that retro and aluminum camper. We had to move or risk withering away as I once did on the third day that I had met my Jay.

I was falling in love with a blue Jay, and distracted I forgot to drink water, to eat, or to sleep under the stars. So, I unknowingly was fading away until I finally fainted. Catching me, as if I were a seed, Jay took me under his wing and placed me in the shade of my desert realty; there is no room for toxicity, remember the lessons of the Joshua Tree; only take what you need, and he chose to take me, the rest was too heavy to carry.

While in that daze of those days, I remembered the day Jay firmly dodged the first time I reached for his chin. In a tent booth full of precious gems and crystals, he was the most captivating -- the most valuable thing. Resonating over the entire Joshua Tree valley, the festival music enveloping the tent seemed muffled and low to the mocking Jay's song. Would he believe that we would spend so many sunrises together in this very desert? Or riding home each sunset before the darkness could envelop the two of us on our motorbikes? One day, although it was sudden, we would fly away. We were unlike the valley's ephemeral blooms, destined instead to flower forever. Nothing was the same after that summer in the desert and, after a year of seasons, we flew away together, my desert Jay and I.

William Walton

William Walton grew up on a ranch in the Texas Hill Country. He graduated from Bandera Texas High School, then from Yale University. A dissolute youth, William tried later to become a deep, sensitive person. It was a waste of time. He spent the rest of his life getting in touch with his innate superficiality, a surprisingly easy task. Except for his work with troubled adolescents, voyaging under sail, and his writing, William never deviated from that path. His stories have been published in An Honest Lie, vols. 2 and 3, anthologies of short stories by Open Heart Publishing, and in Angels on Earth.

The Book of Jake

Jake sat on the shaded porch of his Texas Hill Country home well into his second six-pack of the afternoon. The porch overlooked a lush green pasture, backed by a thick grove of trees where half a dozen cows grazed lazily in the shade. Putting his feet up on the rail, he leaned his rocking chair as far back as it would go, crushing one of several empty cans strewn about the porch floor.

"Hey, Ellie!" he shouted. "How about bringing me a cold beer? I'm almost out."

"Oh no, not out of beer. Anything but that," Ellie answered from the kitchen. "I'll bring you one when I've finished what I'm doing. Or you could just get it yourself if you can still walk."

"Okay, fine, just bring it after you do whatever is so damned important."

"I'm preparing your dinner. Is that important enough for you?"

Great, but why do you have to give me such a hard time about bringing me a friggin' beer? He took another swig.

Turning his attention back to the field, Jake noticed a white light, distinct even in broad daylight, emerging from the trees. The cows began milling around, bellowing fitfully. As the light drew closer, their commotion ceased as abruptly as it had begun. The cows, lowing quietly, seemed drawn into its glow. Docilely, almost in formation, they kept pace as it continued its slow, steady movement toward the house, expanding as it came.

When the light moved so close it obscured everything else from view, Jake saw a figure standing in its midst. He closed his eyes and tried to compose his thoughts, focusing on the smells coming from Ellie's kitchen.

Crap, I've had way, way too much to drink.

When he opened his eyes, he fully expected to find the vision to be gone, but instead it appeared nearer, much too close for comfort.

The figure wore a white robe, which merged with the surrounding light. Its face was that of an older man, but one whose posture was very erect. His long hair and beard were shaggy and unkempt, and he wore a straw hat with its wide brim turned down in front. In his hand he held a gnarled staff with what appeared to be a Harley-Davidson logo on the handle. Despite the almost four foot elevation of the porch, the figure towered head and shoulders above Jake.

"Howdy," said the apparition.

Jake sprang to his feet.

"No, don't get up," said the figure, thrusting his arm forward, the palm of his hand toward Jake. Jake sat back down.

"Who...?" he asked incredulously, his hand trembling so badly he was barely able to hold onto his beer. "Who or what are you?"

"I'm God. Who else?"

"You look more like an over-sized Willie Nelson to me." Jake immediately regretted his remark, hoping he hadn't angered the apparition.

"How'd you get to be such an expert on how I'm supposed to look?" the figure replied. "Besides, now that I think about it, you look a lot like John Belushi. Hey, just joking with you, fella."

"Yeah, very funny. And why should I believe you're God? You could be the friggin' Wizard of Oz as far as I know."

"Well, for openers, who else could appear before you bathed in a bright light? Not your Aunt Emma I'll bet. You ever see a light brighter than this?"

"Okay, yeah, I'll grant you it is pretty damned impressive,"

Jake said, regaining his composure. "Great special effects. Got any other miracles up your sleeve?"

"Well, it just so happens I have a few. Here's a very minor one, just for illustrative purposes. Better put your beer down."

"Why?"

"Just take my word for it."

Jake set his can down on the table next to his chair. The chair began to vibrate, slightly at first, then more roughly.

"Well, Jake, what do you think about that? Not so good on the old hemorrhoids, eh? Yeah, I know you've got them."

Jake burst out laughing.

"Who put you up to this crap?" he said, looking under the chair. "Okay, I don't see any wires. I'm curious how do you do it, but it doesn't really knock my socks off."

Suddenly the chair started rocking so violently Jake had to grip its arms with all his might to keep from being thrown out.

"Yippee! Ride that sucker!" the apparition shouted.

Just when Jake was losing his grip, it stopped.

"I call that my 'Rodeo Cowboy Deluxe,' simple, but effective. Not feeling so skeptical now, are you?"

"N.., no," replied Jake, struggling to catch his breath.

"Good. Unless you want to experience another of my little attention-getters, and believe me I've got some doozies, maybe we can get down to business."

"What do you want from me? Am I in some kind of trouble? Oh, crap, I'm not dying, am I?"

"No, you are not dying, Jake. And you are not in any kind of trouble, unless you've done something I don't know about. Oh, wait a second, I know everything, don't I?"

"Then why would you appear before me?" Jake asked, oblivious to the joke. "I'm nobody special."

"Quite the contrary, you are very special. I have chosen you to demonstrate a love for me, a faith in me, so absolute it shall be spoken of with reverence until the end of time."

"Until the end of time? You gotta be kidding."

"No, not at all. The Book of Jake, your book, will be the first one in the Third Testament of my Holy Bible."

"Book of Jake, my ass. Now I know you're messing with me," Jake said, relaxing slightly. "How are you doing this white light thing anyway? And why aren't you doing it in Vegas for big bucks instead of out here in the boonies? You're every bit as good as that ventriloquist guy who won America's Got Talent. Better maybe. You really had me going there."

"Oh, you think so, do you?" The apparition, without warning, tossed Jake his staff. Jake grabbed at it, lost his grip and fumbled it, but it remained in his hand as if affixed by glue. Jake tried to shake it loose, but could not.

"What the— how the hell did you do that?" Jake asked. The handle of the staff had transformed into the image of a snake's head, turned up with its mouth opened wide. The roof of its mouth was as white as the surrounding light.

"Never mind. Just toss it down on the ground."

"Uh, okay." To Jake's surprise, it fell easily from his hand onto the grass where it turned into a living snake, a very big one. He didn't know what kind it was, but it moved menacingly toward him. Its tail vibrated so rapidly that it made a rustling sound in the leaves. It appeared fully capable of climbing the porch steps. He leapt to his feet.

"It's a water moccasin," the apparition told him. "Cottonmouth. Every bit as poisonous as a rattler."

"Holy friggin' shit, that's...No, I mean, crap, that's one big mother snake."

The apparition chuckled. "That might actually be an understatement." he said.

"Sorry. I was just caught by surprise."

"Forget it. I had to do this with Moses when he doubted his ability to lead his people out of Egypt at my command. Believe me, it got his attention. Have I got yours?"

"Freaking-A, I mean, uh, darned right you have!"

"Good, now grab its tail, pick it up, and toss it back to me." The snake's tail started vibrating again.

"Pick it up? It's a friggin' snake for God's, sake!" Jake caught himself, realizing he had taken the Lord's name in vain. "I'm sorry, I, I didn't mean to blaspheme."

"That's okay. Almost everyone blasphemes when asked to pick up a snake."

Jake smiled feebly. "But you're kidding, right? About picking it up?"

"No, not in the least," the apparition replied. "I'm deadly serious."

"Yeah, that's what I'm afraid of."

"Jake, I command you to pick it up now! I don't think I can put it much more plainly than that. Now!" The air became warmer.

Heart pounding, Jake descended the steps, grabbed the snake by the tail, and it immediately reverted into the rough-hewn wooden staff. He lobbed it back to the apparition who, he was beginning to believe, might indeed be God. Weak-kneed, he stumbled up the steps, and sank into his chair. He gulped down the remnants of his beer, and dropped the can to the floor.

"Ellie," he shouted, turning his head toward the door. "How about bringing me that beer now? Please!" Not only did he badly need one, but he hoped her presence would wake him from this delusion, if that's what it was.

"For God's sake, Jake, I'm trying to fix dinner," Ellie hollered from the kitchen. "Why don't you get off your butt and go fetch it yourself? Not that you haven't already had enough to drink."

"Damn it, Ellie, I don't need you ragging on me right now!"

Ellie came and stood in the doorway. "I'm not ragging on you. I'm working my tail off cooking your meal." Without taking any notice of the apparition, she stepped onto the porch, picked up several beer cans, then walked back into the house.

"Okay, don't get all bent out of shape," Jake shouted after her. "I'll get it myself. Sorry for asking." He didn't know whether to be heartened or shaken that she didn't see the apparition.

Jake reached down, picked up his can, and turned toward the visage. "I gotta go get myself a beer. I suppose I'll have to get you one, too."

"That won't be necessary," the apparition replied, waving his staff. Jake's beer can was instantly full. The unexpected increase in weight startled him, almost causing him to drop it.

"Nice recovery, Jake. Didn't spill a drop. Pretty good reflexes you've got there."

"Yeah, sure. Thanks."

"Don't mention it. I've been filling your beers for years. Haven't you noticed how long it takes you to get through them sometimes? And how you drink better quality beer than you used to?"

"I thought my taste in beer had just evolved. I suppose you were teaching me?"

"Yes, and I am still teaching you. Now maybe we can get down to my business."

"Okay, but first tell me if Moses led his people out of Egypt. I think the Bible says he did, but I'm not sure."

"He did as I instructed. And even when my chosen people strayed and worshipped a false god, I forgave them and delivered them to the promised land. You, too, shall do my will."

"What are you asking of me? I don't have anything in common with Moses," replied Jake, confused.

"You are being way too literal. I only related Moses's story to make a point about certainty of faith. So before I tell you what I require of you, we need to talk about the strength of yours."

"It's pretty strong, I think. I believe in God, I mean you I guess, and all."

"And do you believe that God would ever ask you to do anything wrong?"

"No. Of course not."

"Suppose I asked you to steal food from a convenience store to feed some starving homeless people living under a freeway?"

"Then, I guess I would do as you tell me. But what about the Commandment 'Thou Shalt Not Steal?'"

"I see things that you don't, Jake. You would just have to trust me. Do you think you could do that?"

"I think so, but I wouldn't be comfortable with it. Is that what you want me to do, steal to feed homeless people?" Jake shifted in his seat uneasily.

"No, Jake, but I do require you to demonstrate that your faith in me is absolute."

"Why me?"

"I don't have to explain myself to you. I'm God. Just trust me. Now, are you ready to demonstrate your faith?"

"How?" Jake asked, warily.

"I command you to sacrifice your wife, Ellie."

Jake bolted upright from his chair.

"Holy shit! You want me to what? What do you mean, sacrifice?"

"I want you to slay her."

"Slay? You mean kill her?" Jake began trembling uncontrollably.

The apparition waved his staff and a large knife appeared on the table next to Jake's chair. Jake flinched.

"Yes. Do it now. You can use that knife right there." Jake recoiled from it, backing away several steps.

"Why, in God's name, would I do that?" he asked, wide-eyed.

"To demonstrate the absoluteness of your faith and that your love for me is limitless, as mine is for you."

"I just said I have faith. I never claimed it was like Moses and all those big Bible guys. I'm just a regular person."

"Not anymore. Your testament of faith, as inscribed in the Book of Jake, will be remembered and venerated for all time."

"I don't want to be vener..., venerated."

"Well, you shall be, Jake. Just do as I require of you."

"Please don't ask me to do this!"

"Ask? Did I say ask?" The air got warmer again.

"No. No, I won't!" Tears welled in Jake's eyes.

"You would defy me?" The apparition's tone was now quiet and menacing. It got still warmer, and Jake began to sweat profusely.

"I don't want to disobey you, but I can't do this."

"Yes, you can, Jake. Have faith that God would never lead you astray."

"No, I can't. I'm not killing anybody, and Ellie is the last one on earth that I would harm," Jake said, his eyes narrowing. "The Bible is supposed to be your word, and it says 'Thou Shalt Not Kill.'"

"Yes, and it says 'Thou Shalt Not Steal' too, but you were willing to do that. You either have absolute faith in me or you have none at all."

"Then I have none. No, that's not true, I do have faith, but I don't believe you are God," Jake said. "God would never ask such an awful thing of me." He took several gulps of beer, then set down the can.

"Haven't you read your Old Testament, Jake? When I asked a similar sacrifice of Abraham, the life of his only beloved son, Isaac, he did not refuse. He did not hesitate. He was certain in his faith."

"I don't give a rat's ass what Abraham did. You're not God. I don't know whether you're Satan or just voices in my head, but you sure as hell aren't God. And, if it's voices in my head, I'm not crazy enough to listen to them."

"Abraham had the faith to do as he was told. Now, you shall do the same!"

"No, I won't do it!"

"Jake, obey me now! Your life depends on it. Your eternal one as well." The heat became so intense Jake's shirt was instantly soaked.

Although the sky was perfectly clear, a bolt of lightning struck the ground a few yards from the porch, followed immediately by a tremendous clap of thunder. The pungent smell of smoke filled the air. It was then that Jake had his epiphany.

I'd never do that. I'd rather die than kill Ellie.

Immediately, his fear was lessened to the point that he was almost unaffected by the lightning strike.

"No way," Jake said, picking up his beer. "Get off my property. Now!" Without realizing it, he'd squeezed the can so hard he'd crushed it.

"Defy me at your peril," the apparition said in a quiet, ominous tone.

"Obey you at my peril, you mean, for I would surely rot in hell, or at least state prison, if I did as you command."

"I'm going to say it one last time." The apparition paused. "Trust me," he urged in a less threatening tone.

"No!"

"Well, then, you have determined your own fate, Jake."

The apparition put on his hat and began walking away. A few yards from the porch, he stopped, turned back, and tipped his hat to Jake.

"Know I shall always love you, Jake," he said in a gentle, almost sad, tone, then resumed walking toward the woods, the light receding with him as he went, until he disappeared.

The light continued to fade until it, too, was completely gone, the air cooled, and Jake could see his surroundings again. The cows grazed contentedly, the sun was low in the treetops, and the sky was beginning to pick up the colors of the immanent sunset. He was relieved to see the knife was gone.

Jake needed, really needed, another beer. He stared at the ground where the apparition had stood.

"Okay," he said, picking an empty beer can off the floor and hoisting it. "Make it a Guinness this time."

Nothing happened. Jake realized he'd have to get it himself, that he probably wouldn't get any more freebees. He was fine with that, and got up on wobbly legs to fetch his own. As he opened the front door, Ellie called out to him.

"Honey," she shouted, "dinner is ready. We're having my mother's chicken stew, your favorite."

"Okay, that's great. I'm coming." He struggled to control his trembling as he made his way into the dining room.

"Dinner looks, uh, really good," he said. He held on to the edge of the table, steadying himself for a moment, then, sat down.

Ellie sat down, unfolded her napkin and placed it in her lap. "Do you want to say grace, Jake?"

"No, not tonight."

"Why not?"

"I just don't want to tonight."

"Are you drunk again?"

"I don't know, but that's not it. I just don't want to. I can't."

"Honey, what's wrong?" she asked, her brow furrowing. Jake noticed her eyes were glistening and regretted his earlier unkind remarks had hurt her.

"Nothing I can talk about right now. Just bear with me. I'll explain later."

Jake knew he wouldn't explain later, but with the passage of time he'd be able to say grace again because he didn't believe the apparition had been God. His was a loving and forgiving God. But it might take him awhile. He also knew he would do what he had to if what he experienced had been voices in his head. If they returned, he'd get his shotgun, go into the woods, and shut them up for good. Nothing was ever going to hurt Ellie. Not on his watch. A wave of tenderness washed over him, and he looked across the table at her as though for the first time.

You are the only grace I will ever need, Ellie.

Jake gingerly took his first small bite of her special chicken stew, but his encounter with the apparition had left him with little appetite.

You, Ellie, not any damned chicken stew, are my real favorite dish.

He had hurt her feelings enough today. Things were going to be different from now on.

Jake took a few more bites, pretending to relish them, when he noticed tears running down Ellie's cheeks.

"Ellie, sweetheart, what, what's the matter? Are you, are you...all right?"

"Jake, I..."

Jake felt a sudden tightness in his chest. He struggled, gasping, to catch his breath.

"Ellie, something is, is...very...wrong. I..." Jake stumbled over each word.

He couldn't breathe. The tightness in his chest became a searing pain. His fork fell from his hand, clinked onto his plate, and bounced to the floor. He tried to reach down to pick it up but couldn't move.

"Ellie...help me...please."

"Oh, Jake, I'm so, so sorry," Ellie whispered, wiping at her tears with her napkin. "Please forgive me. I had no choice. God commanded me."

The colored rays of the sunset streamed through the dining room windows and reflected against the opposite wall. The colors seemed first to envelop him, then fill him, and his breathing became less labored. He closed his eyes, a calm came over him, and the image of Ellie's face filled his consciousness.

It's, it's okay, Ellie. I forgive...

THUS ENDED THE BOOK OF JAKE.

Joseph Wilson

Joseph Wilson taught English at King High School for 42 years. His students included Zoe Ramos and Olivia Noble. He writes poetry. He also posts frequently on Facebook, and has a large following.

What I Think I Want This Morning

I want to read the *NewYorkTimesSundayEdition* all the way
through
just once
I want to hear live jazz
in an outdoor city space with the trace of a breeze
and a strong cup
of coffee
I want to walk three miles on the bayfront toward the
Harbor Bridge
I want to go to the restaurant Egg in
Brooklyn and have braised vegetables garnished with fresh herbs
over oatmeal
with a fried egg sunny-side-up
on top
I want to see two movies at the local cinema
which begin at the
same time
I want to gaze into my dog's brown eyes for three minutes
to raise the level of oxytocin in our brains
I want to cut some white roses in the pasture
I want three glasses of Prosecco with raspberries blueberries
and
arils of pomegranate filling the bottom of the bowl of the
wine glass
I want to speak to my mother on the telephone and
have her really be able to hear me
I want to hit some tennis balls with a colleague and raise a

sweat
I want to engage in a serious conversation
face to face with my friend
who can't seem to do that
with me
I want to find just a little mindfulness right now
right now
right now
I want to finish
this poem

Facebook post

Last week I drove to Fort Myers, Florida to drop off a beautiful dog, Arya, and to visit family. I packed two books but didn't think that I would get to them much.

My mistake was that I carried David Lagercrantz's second re-imagining of Stieg Larsson's characters Lisbeth Salander and Mikael Blomkvist. Lisbeth is a top five character all-time in my reading life.

So on my first stop in Mobile I pulled out 2017 "The Girl Who Takes an Eye for an Eye" and read 130 pages. Then I finished the novel in the next two sittings.

While I think this book is the weakest of the Dragon series, Lagercrantz keeps Lisbeth alive and moving forward in my imagination. Lisbeth was an audacious surviving woman before the Metoo@ movement. I love her combination of extreme intelligence and extreme physicality (reminds me of my friend Sue Haag) fighting against the forces of conservative backward thinking. She is a hero for right now.

One thread of the Swedish novel is the disregard and fear of immigrants. The book takes several shots at Trumpthink, which, of course, is an oxymoron.

There are dark and evil men among us.

It is a fast read. If you, like me, like Lisbeth, then take her out for another spin.

***dragon tattoos for quality
***dragon tattoos for likeability

To completely unconstruct the line from "Brokeback Mountain", I am glad that I don't have to quit you, Lisbeth!

Facebook Post

Last night late I finished my 2018 Oscar research by renting "Ladybird" directed by Greta Gerwig from Amazon Prime.

I missed the film on its short run earlier in Corpus. Although it is back again in Corpus Chriisti right now on a big screen with just a few very late viewing times, so I finally saw on my MAC a film that I have read so much about. In addition the wonderful (and not so dying) "NYTimes" has offered video excerpts with technique explanations that have informed me in advance.

This exquisite small film is why I love the movies. Gerwig gives us a peek into the "coming of age" story of Christine or Ladybird (played by the old-soul-in- a-young-body Saoirse Ronan) in Gerwig's own Sacramento setting. Ladybird must as we all must navigate our family's dynamic, high school social structure, and the yearnings of romance and brief attachment.

Ladybird and her mother (Laurie Metcalf) butt heads and words and emotions. Let's face it, the war for separation from our parents is fierce. A lot of love gets spilled here. And a lot of anger and regret.

Both of Ladybird's girl friends are superb, but her boys steal the spotlight. Timothy Chalamet is charming and so gorgeous that who wouldn't fall for him. Lucas Hedges who was so brilliant as the grieving son in "Manchester by the Sea" is just breath-taking as Ladybird's first sweetheart.

The film clocks in at 93 minutes. Gerwig drives a fast car. Believable dialogue, tremendously fleet pacing, and sumptuous photography.

The critics at Rotten Tomatoes score the movie 99 and consumers score it 81. Metacritics give it 94.

*****almost missed proms for quality
*****almost missed proms for likeability

One of the reasons the trope "coming of age" sells so well in the marketplace is that such a vehicle connects with every viewer. Sixty eight year old Joey Wilson is still coming to grips with his own coming of age.

Change with the possibility of growth is the essence of life. I heartily recommend "Ladybird."

It is my pick for Best Film in this year's Oscar race.

Made in the USA
San Bernardino, CA
09 July 2018